WHAT PEOPLE A
ABOUT *SPREAD THE FIRE . . .*

"If you're going to be a Pentecostal, you might as well be a good one. That's the message of Scott Wilson and John Bates in this honest, practical book. Writing humbly, the authors lay out the biblical foundation and pastoral guidance needed to walk people and ministries toward a life continually filled with the Holy Spirit's power. Their book will help you envision how the Holy Spirit can transform your life through a vibrant connection with the Jesus who is the same yesterday, today and forever."

— *Earl Creps, PhD, DMin, lead pastor, church planter, author of* Off-Road Disciplines *and* Reverse Mentoring, *360church.net*

"I am excited about *Spread the Fire* and its potential to motivate pastors toward a new dependence on the person and work of the Holy Spirit in our churches. Scott Wilson and John Bates lead different, yet equally influential, Spirit-filled ministries. However, they share a passion to see the baptism in the Holy Spirit empower believers and strengthen the church for the purpose of winning the lost. These pastors aren't sharing some untested theory—this message reflects what the Spirit is doing in their churches today!"

— *Kermit S. Bridges, DMin, president, Southwestern Assemblies of God University*

"I know personally that the miraculous work of God's Spirit has always been and always will be a fire that can't be contained. In *Spread the Fire*, Scott and John are passionate about their convictions, their struggles, and the answers they've found to the hard questions as Pentecostal pastors in our modern culture. I hope you'll read this book and apply the principles they've outlined. It will make a difference for sure."

— *Dr. Tim R. Barker, superintendent, South Texas District, Assemblies of God*

"Nothing is more critical to the life of the believer than understanding the truth about the baptism in the Holy Spirit. Scott Wilson and John Bates draw attention to the role of today's pastors and leaders to emphasize the baptism in the Holy Spirit as a practical experience in the life of every individual who seeks to know the Lord Jesus Christ in an intimate way. In *Spread the Fire*, the focus is placed on the benefits of this experience and the Spirit's ability to transform every person. I strongly encourage you to read this book, and may the experiences of the New Testament believer be yours as well."

— *Dr. Clarence V. Boyd, Jr., dean of spiritual formation, Oral Roberts University; senior pastor, Revelations-Revealed Truth Evangelistic Center*

"I've been so blessed to watch God use Scott Wilson as a rising voice in our nation, and He continues to use him in the writing of *Spread the Fire*. The baptism in the Holy Spirit is a miraculous work of God. Through the work of the Spirit, amazing things happen. In this book, Scott and John share their convictions, their struggles, and the answers they've found to the hard questions about the Holy Spirit. This book has been a blessing to me and is a must-read for everyone!"

— *Robert Morris, founding senior pastor of Gateway Church, Dallas/Fort Worth, Texas; bestselling author of* The Blessed Life, From Dream to Destiny, The God I Never Knew, *and* Truly Free

"The primary purpose of Spirit-empowerment is to carry out the transformative mission of God among the lost. With the challenges facing the church today, it would be senseless to attempt to effect change in the lives of people merely by utilizing our own ingenuity, intellect, and human effort. God hasn't abandoned us to that fruitless recourse. In *Spread the Fire*, Scott Wilson and John Bates combine the truths of Scripture and the examples of personal testimonies to encourage us to give the Holy Spirit freedom in our personal lives and in our churches. They invite us to allow the Holy Spirit to equip and embolden every believer to confront our lost world with the hope of the gospel."

— *Alton Garrison, assistant general superintendent, The General Council of the Assemblies of God; chairman, Pentecostal Charismatic Churches of North America; co-chair, Empowered 21 USA; author of* Hope in America's Crisis, 360 Degree Disciple, *and* A Spirit-Empowered Church

"We need good theology about the baptism in the Holy Spirit, but we need more than that. We need leaders who are wrestling with the practical ways to impart this teaching—and this vital experience—to men and women, young and old, in today's churches. Scott Wilson and John Bates have given us a tool to help us. Their book is filled with rich biblical insight, as well as practical guides to direct us. With their encouragement, we can trust the Spirit of God to ignite (or reignite) His fire in our lives and our churches."

— *Samuel R. Chand, author of* Leadership Pain: The Classroom for Growth, *www.samchand.com*

"*Spread the Fire* is relevant, biblical, challenging, and practical. Scott Wilson and John Bates deliver a powerful word for twenty-first century believers as they revisit first-century Pentecost and challenge us to embrace all God desires for His church today. Thank you, Scott and John, for being a fresh voice in today's culture to remind us of these truths, and for your call for us to be the Spirit-filled, Spirit-led, and Spirit-empowered church in our communities and around the world."

— *Michael Dickenson, superintendent, New Mexico Ministry Network*

"What a powerful and timely book! In *Spread the Fire*, Scott Wilson and John Bates weave together biblical insight, cultural understanding, and practical wisdom to help you experience a deeper relationship with the Holy Spirit. This is a must-read for anyone who desires a life filled with passion, purpose and a transparent love for God and people. Nothing will revolutionize your prayer life, your study of God's Word, your ministry leadership, or your church more than opening your heart to the work of the Holy Spirit. After reading this book, you will discover a powerful awareness and understanding of how the Holy Spirit moves—and how you can join Him in living out the Pentecostal priority."

— *Kent Ingle, DMin, president, Southeastern University; author of* 9 Disciplines of Enduring Leadership

"Spread the Fire is a compelling call to reclaim the primacy of the Spirit's work in our churches. We can't afford to disciple a generation of churchgoers who have never encountered the power of the Holy Spirit. The question, however, isn't just the doctrinal 'what' but the pastoral 'how.' In this book, John Bates and Scott Wilson shine as both teachers and practitioners as they describe how to lead individuals and congregations into Spirit baptism and Spirit-led living. It's a privilege to know them both. I admire the spiritual leadership they authentically embody."

— *James Bradford, PhD, general secretary, The General Council of the Assemblies of God; author of* Lead So Others Can Follow

"Scott Wilson and John Bates remind us with biblical insight, cultural understanding, and practical experience that the power of the Spirit unleashed at Pentecost is still operative in our churches and our world. *Spread the Fire* is a book of excellent theology, but it's more than that. Wilson and Bates remind us that the life of a church isn't in programs; it's in our experience of the fire of the Holy Spirit—a fire that warms us with comfort and propels us to every corner of our communities and the globe to take the life-changing message of Christ."

— *Rich Wilkerson, Sr., lead pastor, TrinityChurch.TV, Miami, Florida; author of* Inside Out

"I love the axiom, 'From the altars of the past, take the flame and leave the ash.' That is exactly what Scott Wilson and John Bates are emphasizing in their book, *Spread the Fire:* making the baptism in the Holy Spirit integral to the life of the church. Although we are grateful for the way God has poured out His Holy Spirit in the past, we need fresh fire today. The smell of smoke or sight of ashes from days gone by helps no one. This book will inspire individuals and congregations to seek all that God has for them, and once the fire burns anew in them, it will spread to a lost and dying world."

— *Don Meyers, PhD, president, University of Valley Forge*

"Back in the days of no lighters or matches, it was necessary for someone to keep the flame going in the fireplace or red coals burning in the stove for long periods of time. In the winter, letting either go out could mean death. Scott Wilson and John Bates have teamed up to become Spirit-governed 'fire keepers,' who have been charged with never letting the fire on the altar go out. Their book *Spread the Fire* answers practical questions that both the older and younger generations are asking. Reading it will help the older make the transition into 'new wineskins' to hold fresh wine; and it will answer the younger generation's passionate cry, 'Where are all the miracles our ancestors told us about?' "

— *Bishop Walter Harvey, vice president, National Black Fellowship, Assemblies of God; senior pastor, Parklawn Assembly of God, Milwaukee, Wisconsin*

"The book you hold in your hands is an affirmation that the baptism in the Holy Spirit is a privilege for *all* believers. It is a reminder that He (the *person* of the Holy Spirit) plays a critical role in the life and growth of the local church. Scott and John remind us that the transformational power of a church is not in programs; rather, it is found in the active work of the Holy Spirit. I pray that this book will inspire you to seek more 'power' from the Holy Spirit so that you can spread the 'fire' with a greater anointing."

— *Doug Clay, general treasurer, The General Council of the Assemblies of God*

"Scott and John speak out of their own pastoral experiences of realizing that the 'fire was flickering.' Without rekindling the flame, a birthright was in danger. This volume is not an apologetic for a doctrine; instead, it is a passionate plea by pastoral leaders who have the foresight to realize each generation needs to understand Pentecostal faith in their cultural context. The Spirit-empowered life is humble in spirit but confident in the presence and power of the Holy Spirit. We can live in the middle of brokenness, yet be filled with hope. We can experience the turmoil of a dark world, yet live in the light of God's peace."

— *Byron D. Klaus, DMin, president (1999–2015), Assemblies of God Theological Seminary*

"An encouraging must-read for any pastor or leader seeking to consistently pursue the adventure of life in the Spirit within a community of the Spirit."

— *Mike Quinn, lead pastor, New Break, San Diego, California*

"*Spread the Fire* gives us a fresh perspective on first-century Pentecostal reality by dressing it in 2015 clothing. If you want Spirit baptism demystified in a fashion that honors non-Pentecostal traditions while biblically elevating the potency, veracity, and necessity of Spirit baptism and Spirit activity within services and personal lives, then *Spread the Fire* should move to the top of your reading list."

— *Dr. Terry L. Yancey, superintendent, Kansas District, Assemblies of God*

"Spread the word about *Spread the Fire*! It is rock solid in its declaration of the meaning and purpose of the historical view of the baptism in the Holy Spirit. The fire of the Holy Spirit isn't just memory; it can be practiced in the post-modern church. Writing in relevant and contemporary language, Scott and John focus on personal application, so the book is more than a teaching tool. Their message is a call to personal renewal in the Spirit—a call to let this renewal *spread the fire*."

— *Greg Mundis, DMin, executive director, Assemblies of God World Missions*

"At a time when Christians feel increasing pressure to be more private, even individualistic about their faith in Jesus Christ, Scott Wilson and John Bates reassert baptism in the Holy Spirit as the biblical, timeless model for powerful ministry and witness. Passion alone is the low-hanging fruit of Pentecostalism. Scott and John present thoughtful passion conjoined to practice that opens the doors to fresh grace, renewed anointing, and relevance that outlasts the latest media campaign. *Spread the Fire* is a clarion call to all who would resist the temptations of a life or ministry that is domesticated and tame."

— *Michael J. Beals, PhD, president, Vanguard University*

"Scott Wilson and John Bates have tapped into one of the foundational doctrines of the Bible—the Holy Spirit's divine purpose. They're investigative approach to biblical truths about the Holy Spirit (line upon line and precept upon precept) in the church of the twenty-first century is spiritually challenging and enlightening. The insights expressed in *Spread the Fire* explain that the Holy Spirit is the *fire* that makes Jesus, the Savior, known in a spiritual way on earth through His church. I encourage all pastors and church leaders who desire to go to the next level in making Jesus the *supernatural center* of their lives and ministries to read this book, so that none perish."

— *Zollie Smith, executive director, Assemblies of God US Missions*

"All of us want to be part of a movement in which the power of the Holy Spirit impacts our churches and communities. Spirit-empowered Word, worship, work, and witness change everything. In *Spread the Fire,* Scott Wilson and John Bates provide biblical, practical, and applicable insights for church leaders seeking to integrate the presence of the Holy Spirit in their local setting. This book helps pastors and leaders strategically rethink where, when, and how to pursue the experience of the baptism in the Holy Spirit in the contemporary church. The insights of these pastors could be a catalyst for something big in your church!"

— *Tom Jacobs, superintendent, Iowa Ministry Network, Assemblies of God*

"Every generation faces unique challenges as well as new opportunities in carrying out the mission of God in the world. While people and culture constantly change, the strategy for the church in its mission remains the same: the power of the Holy Spirit. We are helpless to reach people with the gospel and transform our communities without a fresh anointing and move of God's Spirit. That's what makes this book so vitally important. Scott Wilson and John Bates remind us that the baptism in the Holy Spirit is available to every believer today, and they reinforce the biblical imperative for the Spirit's work in every part of our lives and in the growth of our churches."

— *Chris Railey, senior director, leadership/church development, The General Council of the Assemblies of God*

"Transparency and passion are evident as Scott Wilson and John Bates share their drift from our Pentecostal distinctive and their call back to renewed desire for the supernatural. They have learned that you can be truly Pentecostal and culturally authentic at the same time. They emphasize the importance of the manifestation of the supernatural gifts operating in their growing congregations, and they provide practical, organic ways to reintroduce these opportunities. This book will create a hunger for fresh anointing with evidence that miracles still happen today."

— *Larry Liebe, superintendent, Wisconsin/Northern Michigan Ministries Network*

"Relevance doesn't have to be synonymous with compromise. Indeed, the Holy Spirit, who speaks in a language all can understand, lures us into the most relevant form of Christianity: living out the Scripture in our cultural context. In this clear message and clarion call, Scott and John remind us that the power of the Holy Spirit is profound and practical for both the church *individual* and the church *corporate*. I recommend this book, and even more I recommend the spiritual encounter they so beautifully describe."

— *Heath Adamson, senior director of youth ministry, The General Council of The Assemblies of God; author of* The Bush Always Burns

"Traveling the globe, I've experienced the powerful seen and unseen manifestations of the work of the Spirit. But a defiant, unbelieving culture—with its tough questions and harsh judgments—is pervasive. And the modern church has drifted away from teaching on Holy Spirit baptism and its physical manifestations such as speaking in tongues. In *Spread the Fire*, Scott Wilson and John Bates provide practical ways to reignite the importance of this vital experience in our own lives and in our churches. This fiery apologetic is infused with Spirit-drenched wisdom that will refresh your heart and renew your commitment to lead in the power of the Holy Spirit."

— *Rob Hoskins, president of OneHope*

"In a period of history when the power of programs holds sway over the power of Holy Spirit, the presence of men replacing the presence of God's Spirit, and strange fire filling our altars, Scott Wilson and John Bates address the church's drift away from the perspective of the early church and advocate the return to our basics. They acknowledge the dilemma we face in introducing and interpreting the Holy Spirit to a techno-savvy generation that has shied away from Him. They don't advocate returning to modes of the past, but instead, they encourage us to develop methods of communicating this vital life of the church in culturally relevant, socially non-threatening, and currently viable ways."

— *Chadwick Mohan, lead pastor, New Life Assemblies of God Church (NLAG), Chennai, India*

"In *Spread the Fire*, Scott Wilson and John Bates help us in two ways: They encourage us to find and use the fire from the true altar of heaven, and they warn us to avoid using earthly fire rather than the Holy Spirit to build the church. I know both of these men and their stories. Both of them have watched their churches increase. They've made sure they are operating with heavenly fire and are giving the Holy Spirit room to be God. It's never too late to become a Spirit-empowered, Spirit-led church!"

— *Rick DuBose, superintendent, North Texas District, Assemblies of God*

"In so many areas of life, 'old school' is becoming 'new school' again. As my wife, Valery, and I travel the globe working with movements and with leaders, one of the resounding themes is that 'the Holy Spirit is making a comeback!' *Spread the Fire* gives contemporary application to the Ancient of Days in the person of the Holy Spirit. Thank you, Scott and John, for this significant contribution to the modern church."

— *Michael Murphy, founding director, Leaderscape*

"This topic is incredibly important to the life of every believer; yet comparatively little has been written recently about how the baptism in the Holy Spirit can impact our lives and the effectiveness of our churches. I'm thrilled that Scott Wilson and John Bates have given us such practical and powerful insight on this vital relationship with God. I highly recommend this book to anyone and everyone interested in all God has for them."

— *Jeff Leake, lead pastor, Allison Park Church, author of* God in Motion *and* Praying With Confidence

"Most all pastors want an outpouring of God's Holy Spirit. Some passionately petition heaven for that outpouring. Fewer, however, are bold enough to allow God to sovereignly move when and how He desires. In *Spread the Fire*, Scott and John provide a scriptural framework as well as a practical picture of what it looks like for a ministry to truly be Spirit-led."

— *Scotty Gibbons, strategist, National Youth Ministries of The Assemblies of God*

"The Assemblies of God is profoundly a Pentecostal fellowship. Its birth pangs came over 100 years ago in the spiritual fires of the early twentieth-century outpouring, and that outpouring continues unabated to this day. However, a new generation is now confronted with the challenge of proclaiming, defending, and practicing this key element of our faith. Scott and John challenge us to understand that not only the message but the 'container' that delivers the message needs to be in focus if a new generation is to embrace and engage our distinctive role as a fellowship. Pentecost must be more than our heritage; it must be our practice and experience today."

— *James R. Braddy, superintendent, Northern California Nevada District, Assemblies of God*

SCOTT WILSON & JOHN BATES

SPREAD THE FIRE

SPIRIT BAPTISM IN TODAY'S CULTURE

GPH®

Gospel Publishing House

DEDICATION

From Scott ...

I dedicate this book to my dad, Dr. Tom Wilson, who prayed with me to receive the baptism in the Holy Spirit when I was eight-years-old. Thank you for praying with me, praying for me, and modeling what a Spirit-empowered prayer life looks like. I will never forget our early morning, family prayer meetings. Thank you for making me get out of bed!

From John ...

I dedicate this book to my father, O. C. Bates, who lost his battle with cancer in May of 2015. My father was thoroughly Pentecostal in his convictions, life, pastoring, and preaching. It is from this Pentecostal heritage I have gleaned much of my experience and knowledge regarding the workings of the Holy Spirit. The person of the Holy Spirit was made real to me through Dad's teachings and obedience to the voice of the Holy Spirit in church settings. It was not until years later I was able to discern what I had learned. I was taught the Holy Spirit is not a person to fear, He is my friend.

CONTENTS

FOREWORD

When I was growing up, church wasn't just a Sunday-morning affair. You attended church Sunday morning, Sunday night, Wednesday night, and—when revivals hit town—every night of the week. You always knew when a worship service began, but you never knew when it might end. That depended on the all-important business God was transacting with people at the altar.

Today, Christians spend far less time at church. Sunday-night services are becoming a thing of the past for many congregations, and attendance is down at midweek services. Churches often have multiple Sunday morning worship services, which necessitate programming each service down to the minute. You always know when the service begins, and you're pretty confident when it will end too.

These changes in church life reflect changes in culture. Some people work long hours or multiple jobs. At night, they want to come home and rest from a busy, stressful day. Others have kids who are enrolled in extracurricular sports, and their team's practice schedule conflicts with the church's calendar. All of us have been conditioned by society's "microwave mentality," which believes that good things come to those who . . . push buttons. The concept of waiting for something good—*tarrying* in the old-time church language I grew up with—is foreign to them.

We could look at these changes in church life and conclude that they ought to be resisted. From this point of view, multiple weekly worship services that last well into the evening are the means God uses to do His work. Cutting back on services hinders God's work. There's a lot to be said for this point of view, including the fact that it produced us.

We could also look at these changes and conclude that they ought to be accommodated. In this perspective, multiple weekly worship services are a means of accomplishing the desired end, but not the only way. To use an analogy, you can heat your living room with a gas burning or a wood-burning fireplace. What's important is the fire, not the fireplace.

Scott Wilson and John Bates use the image of fire to talk about the baptism in the Holy Spirit that Jesus Christ promised believers. They are thoroughgoing Pentecostals who desire a fresh move of the Holy Spirit in the lives of individuals, churches, and nations. They are also pastors of creative churches who recognize that the means and methodologies of a previous generation don't always work in this generation. They're more interested in the fire than the fireplace.

I commend this book to you, not because you will necessarily agree with Scott and John's every proposal. You won't. They have their own disagreements about some of these matters. Rather, I commend this book to you because it wrestles with how to kindle the flame of Pentecost in a new culture among a new generation.

— *George O. Wood is general superintendent of
the Assemblies of God (USA) and chairman
of the World Assemblies of God Fellowship*

1 DAMP WOOD

What the Church needs today is not more machinery or better, not new organizations or more and novel methods, but men whom the Holy Ghost can use, men of prayer, men mighty in prayer. The Holy Ghost does not flow through methods, but through men. He does not come on machinery, but on men. He does not anoint plans, but men, men of prayer.

—E. M. Bounds

IN RECENT YEARS, REPORTS, INSIDE AND OUTSIDE THE ASSEMBLIES of God, show that the public practice of speaking in tongues "has come under certain scrutiny."[1] The problem isn't theology. In our fellowship, the vast majority of pastors and church leaders affirm the theological teaching about the baptism in the Holy Spirit and the initial physical evidence of tongues; the problem is in the practice . . . or more accurately, the lack of practice.

In an article for *Christianity Today*, Cary McMullen explains that the fellowship is experiencing "an identity crisis," which, ironically, is the result, in his opinion, of several very positive factors, including significant growth in numbers and influence in AG churches. So the movement is growing as the expression of gifts has declined.

Also, many other denominations and independent churches have moved toward more expressive worship. These factors have essentially eroded the distinctive nature of the Assemblies of God. A 2008 survey of AG pastors revealed that 90 percent teach regularly on the baptism in the Holy Spirit, but only 28 percent provide regular time for people in their churches to receive the baptism in the Spirit. In addition, only half of those who attend worship claim to be baptized in the Holy Spirit. The first number, the one about pastors, has probably remained the same, but the other two have probably declined even more over the past few years.

General Superintendent George O. Wood explains a primary reason why the frequency of speaking in tongues in public settings has become limited in recent years. "There's been a cultural shift in the last thirty years," he notes. "Sunday morning services used to be for believers, and Sunday night services were more evangelistic. Sunday night services have declined, and now the morning service is more for people to bring friends. If there has been a diminution of the gift, it's due to a cultural shift in society."[2]

These factors have dampened the wood God wants to use to create a magnificent, Spirit-ignited fire among us. The Scriptures describe different kinds of baptism: in water and in fire. In one, we get wet; in the other, we get hot. The problem isn't that our pastors and church leaders suddenly have a clouded or erroneous biblical understanding about the baptism in the Holy Spirit. Many have simply drifted from our historical roots in their public practice.

Fire is a powerful metaphor in the Scriptures. Many of the times the word is used, it means a literal fire, but when it is used symbolically, it has a rich lexical range. It sometimes refers to God's righteous judgment, such as John's reference in Revelation to his vision of Jesus with "eyes like blazing fire" (Rev. 1:14). First and more often, however, it refers to the presence and glory of God, even as a theophany. God appeared to Moses in the burning bush (Ex. 3:2–6) and at Mt. Sinai (Ex. 19:18) and to the people over the tabernacle in the wilderness (Num. 9:15). In the New Testament, Paul describes the return of Christ "in blazing fire" (2 Thess. 1:7), which combines the concepts of His presence and His judgment. John the Baptist predicted Jesus, the Messiah, would baptize people "with the Holy Spirit and fire" (Matt. 3:11 and Luke 3:16), a promise fulfilled on the day of Pentecost as the 120 disciples were filled with the Spirit and "tongues of fire" descended on them (Acts 2:3–4). This was the physical and dramatic manifestation of the Holy Spirit in the lives of the first believers, the impartation of God's presence and power to fulfill His purposes.[3] It is *this* fire that we are describing in this book.

The fire of God's presence and power is no less important (and no less available) today. In a revealing article for *Christianity Today*, Ed Stetzer observes that the baptism in the Spirit is a dividing line between passionate devotion and lukewarm church membership:

In almost all Pentecostalism . . . speaking in tongues follows the Holy Spirit's baptism. After that experience, it's hard to say, "Oh I don't take this whole thing serious, I don't even know if it's real." When you believe you're speaking in another language, that belief reshapes the way you think about faith! Being a nominal Presbyterian, Methodist, or Baptist is easier; though there are some outward expectations like baptism . . . that can mark a spiritual commitment. But Pentecostal believers and churches constantly emphasize spiritual practice and engagement. That helps make a more robust faith. So, more often than not, stagnation is not as compatible with a real Spirit-filled experience.[4]

A LOOK BACK

We stand in a long, powerful, and fascinating history of the use of the gifts, including the traditional Pentecostal movement, a later Charismatic movement, and the Third Wave. In 1900, Charles Parham opened a Bible School in Topeka, Kansas. While Parham was away speaking at an event, his students studied Luke's account of Pentecost in Acts 2. They worshiped God and prayed together for several days. On the night of January 1, 1901, one of the students, Agnes Ozman, requested the students lay hands on her, asking Jesus to baptize her in the Holy Spirit and then she began to speak in tongues. When Parham returned, he began teaching others about the baptism in the Spirit, but he encountered significant opposition and his ministry disintegrated.

Two years later in El Dorado Springs, Missouri, Parham began preaching about God's healing power. God worked in powerful ways, and hundreds showed evidence of healing. Parham's ministry soon expanded throughout Kansas, Oklahoma, and Texas. In Houston, he opened a

Bible school. One of those who attended was William J. Seymour, who soon became the pastor of an "apostolic faith assembly."

In 1905, an African-American woman named Neely Terry attended a holiness church in Los Angeles. When she traveled that year to visit her family in Houston, Texas, she visited a church pastored by William Seymour. Terry invited Seymour to come to Los Angeles to preach at her church. He arrived in February the next year. After preaching and praying for five weeks, one man, Edward S. Lee, began speaking in tongues. At the next meeting, six more spoke in tongues.

> **Whites, African-Americans, and Hispanics of every economic class came to hear Seymour and others preach and, of course, to observe those who were speaking in tongues and shouting praises to God.**

News quickly spread throughout the city. Whites, African-Americans, and Hispanics of every economic class came to hear Seymour and others preach and, of course, to observe those who were speaking in tongues and shouting praises to God. A neighbor near the church reported, "They shouted three days and three nights. It was Easter season. The people came from everywhere. By the next morning there was no way of getting near the house.

As people came in they would fall under God's power; and the whole city was stirred. They shouted until the foundation of the house gave way, but no one was hurt."[5]

After the front porch of the building collapsed from the weight of the crowd, the church moved to Azusa Street to a building previously used by an African Methodist Episcopal church. Only a few weeks after the first evidence of speaking in tongues, between 300 and 1,500 people were coming for worship to different services. The congregation was wonderfully ecumenical, including Baptists, Presbyterians, Quakers, and Mennonites. By the end of the year, many other congregations had been birthed from the original group. Several existing holiness denominations adopted the teaching about speaking in tongues.

One of the people who experienced the baptism in the Holy Spirit at Azusa Street was a single lady, Rachel Sizelove. She traveled home to visit her family in Springfield, Missouri, and she led them in a prayer meeting. Several of them were baptized in the Holy Spirit. Rachel was a member of the Corum family who were the founders of what is now Central Assembly of God in Springfield, Missouri.

As the fire spread over the next few years, it became apparent that the movement needed better organization. In April of 1914, about 300 leaders met in Hot Springs, Arkansas, to clarify doctrinal positions, encourage unity, and chart a course of worldwide evangelistic outreach and church planting. This became the first General Council of the Assemblies of God. The fire of the Spirit was evident in the churches that formed the fellowship. The preaching called people to follow God with all their hearts and repent of every sin. People spoke in tongues in worship services, others interpreted, and prophecies were given. Worship was loud and demonstrative.

In the 1930s, our fellowship held Prayer and Bible Conferences. During these events, the only agenda was listening to the Lord and obeying Him. No speakers were scheduled. Those who attended prayed and responded to the prompting of the Spirit. There were spontaneous preaching and spontaneous prayer meetings. After a few years, the event lost its distinctive. It became a carefully planned conference of scheduled speakers with far less prayer.

In the fifties, some Pentecostal evangelists held "healing revivals" in all parts of the country. Sadly, a few of these leaders crossed the lines of theology and practice. In light of these excesses, many pastors of local churches withdrew support for them by the 1960s.

In the decade of the '60s, T. F. Zimmerman became General Superintendent of the General Council of the Assemblies of God and brought many updates and changes to the movement. Our fellowship became accepted in the National Association of Evangelicals. In many ways, we had arrived and found our place in the mainstream of American church culture. Our movement became more organized, and we grew rapidly.

In the '60s and '70s, the emphasis on the gifts spread beyond the traditional Pentecostal denominations and fellowships to mainline denominations and even to Roman Catholic and Orthodox churches. Some pastors and priests encouraged the experience of the gifts, but often, these were lay-led, Charismatic movements. Pockets of people within these churches who were hungry for more of God were baptized in the Holy Spirit, experienced the gifts, and encouraged one another in prayer meetings and small groups. At the same time, the exuberant Jesus Movement swept college campuses and the youth culture. All of this confused many people in established Pentecostal churches. It seemed odd to have a priest in robes or young people in shorts and tank tops laying hands on people, being baptized in the Holy Spirit, and speaking in tongues.

Gradually, the movement spread and found different expressions in Reformed and dispensational churches. Many of these leaders and church members came to believe in the miraculous gifts and signs, but they didn't believe speaking in tongues was essential or an initial physical evidence of the baptism in the Holy Spirit. This movement, labeled "Third Wave" by Fuller Seminary professor C. Peter Wagner, focused on the personal experience of the presence and power of the Spirit, with or without any physical manifestation. In these churches, all the gifts in 1 Corinthians 12 were as important as tongues. There was no emphasis on a prayer language being available to all people. They also taught that conversion and the baptism in the Spirit were considered to be simultaneous events.

CHANGING TRADITIONS

All Assemblies of God credentialed ministers believe and defend the classic Pentecostal theology of the baptism in the Holy Spirit and the initial physical evidence of speaking in tongues. However, changes in our culture have affected the actual practice in church services, as well as when and how the baptism in the Spirit is taught to those who are interested.

Traditionally, Sunday night services were the time and place where people were invited to be baptized in the Spirit. In fact, Sunday nights were often as well attended in our movement as Sunday morning, and sometimes even more people came in the evening. Today, many churches no longer meet on Sunday nights. According to the 2013 study of Assemblies of God churches, the attendance on Sunday evenings is only about one-sixth of the attendance for Sunday morning worship.[6] Only a few decades ago, virtually every church had "evangelistic services" on Sunday nights. After worship and the sermon, the pastor would give the initial altar call to invite people to respond to his gospel message. Many people got saved, but that was only the beginning of the service. The next part included expression of the gifts and another altar call for those who were seeking the baptism in the Spirit or simply more of God. It was open-ended and the gifts of the Spirit flowed freely.

These prolonged evenings were often called "tarrying services" because people waited on the Lord to show up in power. Children usually attended these services with their parents. If they got sleepy, they curled up on the pews or in their parents' laps. For them, these long and exciting services were part of their spiritual heritage.

In this part of the service, the pastor didn't do a lot of teaching, but he and the people did a lot of praying. At some point, the pastor invited people to come forward. When they came, others gathered around them, laid hands on them, and prayed. The Lord moved; they were baptized in the Holy Spirit, and spoke in tongues. In those years, if you attended an Assemblies of God church in Massachusetts, a church in Florida, or a church in California, you saw virtually the same activities on any Sunday night.

Gradually, over the past three decades, the Sunday evening services have become inconvenient and seemingly irrelevant. For many people who attend our churches, perceptions and priorities have changed. They have concluded that the services lasted too long. Many parents had to get up early for long commutes to work, kids had to go to bed because they had school the next day, and mobility caused some people to move far away from family members who might take care of the kids so the adults could stay in the service.

Sunday morning isn't normally an environment conducive to calling for people to be baptized in the Holy Spirit.

Sunday evening services no longer worked well for the purpose they had served for generations. Today, people usually attend a single service on a weekend (if they go to church at all). For this reason, Sunday morning isn't normally an environment conducive to calling for people to be baptized in the Holy Spirit. Far from being willing to tarry, people are looking at the clock. They want to get out on time so they can get to their favorite restaurant before the Baptists and Methodists, or they want to get home to watch the beginning of the game ... or take a nap. If a pastor had an altar call for people to come down for extended prayer and to be baptized in the Spirit, many wouldn't feel comfortable down front praying, and those watching from the pews would feel anxious as the scheduled time for the end of the service came and went. Waiting is hard enough for members, but it feels especially awkward for visitors—and for those who brought them. Nursery and childcare workers are looking at the clock, too. They're eager for parents to relieve them of their duties.

All of this produces a conundrum for pastors who want their people to experience the baptism in the Spirit, speak in tongues, and express other gifts in worship. In a culture that rushes Sunday morning worship and avoids Sunday evening service, how does the church give people the opportunity to be baptized in the Holy Spirit? There has to be an answer.

COMMON FEARS

Pastors can easily identify many real fears of what might happen if they allow time on Sunday morning to instruct and invite people to be baptized in the Holy Spirit. We can at least list a few of them:

- New people (and some who have been coming fewer than thirty years) will feel awkward when the gifts are expressed—and some of them probably won't come back.

- Pastors will either need to rush the process to get done on time, or the service will go much longer than the scheduled time to end. Neither of these options works.

- If people feel rushed, they won't feel comfortable and open to the Spirit. Instead, they'll feel pressured, frustrated, and guilty when they don't have the experience they expected and the pastor promised.

- If a pastor decides to have a tarrying service on Sunday morning, he may announce, "If you need to leave, you can, but those who want to experience the baptism in the Spirit can stay after the service." This may seem like a reasonable solution, but it can set up a two-tiered spirituality: Those who stay are "more than," and those who leave are "less than." We already have enough trouble with church unity. It's not a good idea to inflame superiority and inferiority!

- If the nursery and childcare workers have to stay until the extended service is over in thirty minutes or an hour, they may not want to sign up for the next year (or come back the next week). And if parents are told they have to go pick up their kids while the service continues, many of them just won't come back because it's too hard to press in at the altar while taking care of children.

These fears are very real to pastors and other church leaders, and they raise questions that aren't easily answered.

MAYBE NOT REALLY NECESSARY

Ironically, as the emphasis on public expression of the gifts has waned, our fellowship has continued to grow. People are coming to Christ, missionaries are being sent out, churches are being planted, worship is alive and beautiful, and people are studying their Bibles. In light of the complexities of finding a way to fit in the teaching and experience of the baptism in the Spirit, this practice may seem less than absolutely essential for an already vibrant, growing church.

> **The forces of a changing culture and time pressures have slowly, inexorably eroded the emphasis on the baptism in the Spirit and the expression of tongues.**

Our pastors regularly pray in the Spirit. Praying in tongues and using the other gifts are essential to their spiritual vitality, and they firmly uphold the theological position that is a pillar of our movement. However, the forces of a changing culture and time pressures have slowly, inexorably eroded the emphasis on the baptism in the Spirit and the expression of tongues.

This teaching and these opportunities, though, haven't completely vanished. Many pastors feel comfortable and confident that the teaching on the baptism in the Spirit is included in youth camps and in discipleship training classes or small groups. In this way, this teaching happens about three times a year in many churches. These pastors have concluded that these venues and the frequency of them are good ways to make room for this experience. But is it enough?

Some leaders have noticed the absence of fire in Assemblies of God churches in America. In a powerful talk at the Assemblies of God Centennial Celebration, Dick Brogden, a missionary to the Arab world, spoke of the heart of the Pentecostal experience. If we're not careful, he warned, we'll seek the gifts instead of the Giver:

> The cardinal doctrine of Pentecost is *more*, but not just more of personal power, but more of Jesus. Pentecostal power is rooted in the person of Jesus. The Spirit glorifies Christ. Spirit baptisms are further steps into the knowledge of God whereby Jesus becomes more real to the soul. When men and women linger in the presence of Jesus—when we hunger and thirst and when we ache for more of Jesus—Jesus comes to us, Jesus abides with us, Jesus baptizes us with His precious Holy Spirit. The power we are clothed with by the Spirit is not mechanical energy. Power alone ironically tends to take us away from Jesus. Pentecost is the power of divine life imparted to us by the Spirit through intimacy with the divine Son. When Jesus is all that thrills the soul, He cannot be contained in the heart. He swells in our spirits; He bursts forth from our tongues. When Jesus is all that we want, we find that He is all that we need. Being full of Him,

we stand in front of men and women with faces shining and eyes piercing and tongues praising. It is the ongoing experience and reality of Jesus that empowers our witness.

Brogden explained that our focus needs to return to its rightful place:

We don't seek signs. We don't seek wisdom. We don't seek tongues. We seek the unbroken wonder of being lost in the presence of Jesus. Jesus is our power. Jesus is our sign. Jesus is our wisdom. Jesus is our tongue. Jesus is our distinctive. Jesus is our focus. Jesus is our wonder. Jesus is our life. Jesus is our all. And if we as a movement will return to the simplicity of just having Jesus, we will obey the Great Commission.

Through personal observation and in meetings with leaders around the world, Brogden heard that America—and America's church—has lost its priorities. Church leaders from other countries who visit our nation shouldn't be fooled by our large buildings, beautiful music, and perfectly planned programs. He addressed the visitors from other lands: "For the wind of Pentecost now blows and the fires of mission now rage, not from us to thee, but from thee to us.... Don't condemn us to be only the funders and donors for the gospel as you suffer and die for its advance. If we are relegated only to supporting your sacrifice, we are of all men most pitiful."[7]

Some who heard Brogden's message that night might have been offended by his remarks, but after he spoke,

Dr. Wood told the gathering, "We receive this as a prophetic utterance. God has spoken to us tonight, and we cannot ignore it."

WHAT NOW?

Pastors face a dilemma. One pastor told us, "I don't have any problem with the theology of our movement. I believe it, and I embrace it. I speak in tongues in my private prayers. It's a vital part of my walk with God. In fact, I don't know what my spiritual life would be without it. But here's the truth: most of the people who have joined our church aren't from a Pentecostal background. They come for wonderful worship and, I hope, some good preaching. I talk about the gifts, but it looks like they're confused. I don't know what to do. If I make it more of an emphasis, I'm afraid I'll lose them. Our church seems to be doing fine without emphasizing the baptism in the Spirit and tongues."

Another pastor voiced an even more common problem: "I really want our people to experience the fullness of the Spirit. It's not something that's less important than any other priority in our church, but I can't figure out how to make it fit in our schedule and make it meaningful. I tried changing our midweek service to be more like the Sunday night services we experienced in the past. The first few weeks were fairly well attended—like all events that get started at our church. But after a month, everyone who wanted to be baptized in the Spirit had already come. Families didn't show up, and young people were at youth group. We limped along for a few more weeks, and then we went back to classes and small groups. I just can't see it happening on Sunday morning. For many reasons, it would be a disaster! I have some older men on our board who wonder why we don't go back to 'the old ways,' and I have some younger men who don't understand why it's such a big deal. At this point, I need some help. I feel discouraged, and to be honest, a little guilty because I'm not leading our people in an experience I think is vital for them."

Our fathers and grandfathers wouldn't recognize what's going on in many of our churches today. They expected to have two vibrant services: one Sunday morning for preaching and worship and one Sunday night for evangelism, the baptism in the Spirit, and the flow of the gifts. It's obvious, though, that many pastors are finding it extremely difficult to figure out how to make this experience real for every believer in their congregations.

We're not recommending that we turn back the clock and go back to the old ways. We need something new, something ancient in power and purpose but contemporary in availability, relevance, and practice. Is that even possible? Yes, we believe it is.

At the end of each chapter, you'll find a few questions to stimulate your thinking, warm your heart, and encourage conversations with other pastors and leaders in your church. We're not offering easy answers. We're inviting you to ask the Lord to give you all you need. He will.

How long has it been in many of our
churches since God "did awesome things
that we didn't expect"? What stops us
today from drawing a line in the sand
and setting our hearts toward God in
fervent prayer that he will come and
revive his work in us as well as in our
churches? Why don't we stop rationaliz-
ing and justifying the spiritual impotence
all around us? Why not rather humble
ourselves and seek God with all our
hearts for "something from heaven"?

—Jim Cymbala

CONSIDER THIS . . .

1. How have you understood the similarities and differ-
    ences in the Pentecostal movement, the Charismatic
    movement, and the Third Wave?

2. What are some reasons having anything resembling a "tarrying meeting" no longer works on Sunday nights ... or Sunday mornings?

3. What do you hope to get out of this book? What are you expecting God to do for you, in you, and through you?

2 MORE OF GOD

Spirit-filled souls are ablaze for God. They love with a love that glows. They serve with a faith that kindles. They serve with a devotion that consumes. They hate sin with fierceness that burns. They rejoice with a joy that radiates. Love is perfected in the fire of God.

—Samuel Chadwick

WE'RE NOT SUGGESTING THAT ANY PASTOR CHANGE DIRECTION for the sake of history. Past experiences and legacies can inform, but they shouldn't dictate. Our decisions as pastors have to be Spirit-directed, and they have to make sense to us, our leaders, and our congregations. In past years, people assumed pastors had a lot of authority in their lives. If a pastor told them something would be good for them, they didn't ask many questions. They just embraced it. After Watergate, the authority of leaders was shattered in some arenas and eroded in others. The church has seen a significant erosion of the authority of the pastor in the eyes of many. A survey by Gallup shows a 20 percent decline, a record low, in trust of pastors over the last two decades, ranking in trustworthiness below nurses, pharmacists, grade-school teachers, medical doctors, military officers, and police officers.[8] To establish and reinforce trust, pastors need to take more time to explain the reasons and the benefits of any course we recommend.

ESSENTIAL

In the early years of the Pentecostal movement, spiritual power was considered essential for anyone who applied for a leadership position. Our founders looked at Acts 6 when the apostles realized they couldn't do all the leadership and administration necessary for a growing church. In response to unmet needs and complaints, they told the people, "It would not be right for us to neglect the ministry of the word of God in order to wait on tables. Brothers and sisters, choose seven men from among you who are known to be full of the Spirit and wisdom. We will turn this responsibility over to them and will give our attention to prayer and the ministry of the word" (Acts 6:2–4). The ones who served in administrative capacities weren't second-class believers. They needed to be people who were "full of the Spirit and wisdom."

Luke emphasizes the charismatic gifts as a practical reality in the lives of believers. In his book, *The Charismatic Theology of St. Luke*, Roger Stronstad remarks, "To the extent that Luke makes it explicit, the charismatic gift of the Holy Spirit in Luke-Acts is always an experiential phenomenon. Throughout Luke-Acts the gift of the Spirit for vocation is never a matter of faith-perception, but is always an experience-reality."[9]

As movements age, the initial zeal, intensity, and purity often becomes diluted by attempts to organize all the priorities and activities. After a while, leaders and their people can easily lose the passion and vision, and they settle for administrative order. Virtually all great movements go through these stages. From time to time, reform efforts try to return those who will listen to the original passion and vision.

To some degree, and in some corners, this drift has happened in our movement. Too often, the baptism in the Spirit and the experience of tongues have become only a badge of honor for our members and an entry pass for anyone who aspires to be a pastor, a leader, or a teacher. In these cases, the expression of gifts is a ticket to a place at the leadership table, not evidence of the fire of personal, spiritual fervor.

For instance, a pastor may need seven people for his board (or Sunday school teachers or any other leadership roles in the church). When he interviews them, he may find that only five of the leading candidates have experienced the baptism in the Spirit. Out of organizational necessity, he leads a meeting to invite a few more leaders to be baptized in the Spirit, but it's out of administrative necessity. To qualify for the positions, they only need to claim they've had the initial experience; they're not required to embody the fruit that comes from a Spirit-empowered life.

For some pastors, especially for those who served a generation or two ago, teaching people about the baptism in the Holy Spirit seems to take away the mystery. In the early years of our movement, the fire was so powerful that people experienced the baptism in the Spirit only by laying hands on them and praying for them, totally apart from any cogent and careful teaching on the doctrines and practice. This still happens in many parts of the world, such as South America, Asia, and Africa, because people there don't have layers of suspicion of authority. It's easier to be baptized in fire when there's a fire blazing in every church service you attend. To them, it's as new and fresh and real as it was on the day of Pentecost, the first days of Azusa Street, and the first General Council.

THE FIRE, NOT THE GIFTS

The gifts are demonstrable, they are evident, and they are personal. It's easy for us to focus on the expression of tongues that comes as a result of the baptism in the Spirit, but our spiritual eyes need to be riveted on the fire, not the gifts. Before Jesus came to him at the Jordan River, John the Baptist explained to his followers, "I baptize you with water. But one who is more powerful than I will come, the straps of whose sandals I am not worthy to untie. He will baptize you with the Holy Spirit and fire" (Luke 3:16).

> It's easy for us to focus on the expression of tongues that comes as a result of the baptism in the Spirit, but our spiritual eyes need to be riveted on the fire, not the gifts.

Of course, the first and dramatic evidence of this fire occurred on Pentecost. Luke tells us, "When the day of Pentecost came, they were all together in one place.

Suddenly a sound like the blowing of a violent wind came from heaven and filled the whole house where they were sitting. They saw what seemed to be tongues of fire that separated and came to rest on each of them. All of them were filled with the Holy Spirit and began to speak in other tongues as the Spirit enabled them" (Acts 2:1-4).

Tongues are important, but they are the result, not the cause of spiritual vitality. They are the smoke; the Holy Spirit is the fire. As an aging, growing, expanding movement, we need to keep our eyes on the source of power and love.

DIVINE PRESENCE

Before Jesus ascended, He spent forty days teaching His followers. After the resurrection, He appeared to Mary, the Eleven, the two on the road to Emmaus, Peter and the others after a night of fishing, and more than 500 people at one time (1 Cor. 15:6). In an account that parallels Matthew's Great Commission passage, Mark records Jesus' rebuke, challenge, and commission of the Eleven:

Later Jesus appeared to the Eleven as they were eating; he rebuked them for their lack of faith and their stubborn refusal to believe those who had seen him after he had risen.

He said to them, "Go into all the world and preach the gospel to all creation. Whoever believes and is baptized will be saved, but whoever does not believe will be condemned. And these signs will accompany those who believe: In my name they will drive out demons; they will speak in new tongues; they will pick up snakes with their hands; and when they drink deadly poison, it will not hurt them at all; they will place their hands on sick people, and they will get well." (Mark 16:14–18)[10]

We like to read the last part of this passage, but we need to pay attention to the first part, too. Most of us have said or thought, "If I could just see Jesus and hear His voice, my questions would be answered and I'd have great faith." But look at the disciples. They were with Him for over three years, and they saw the resurrected, glorified Savior for almost six weeks, but they still had a "lack of faith" and "stubborn refusal to believe" in His resurrection—even though He was standing right in front of them!

What does it mean, then, to be full of faith and to believe in the glorified Savior who died and rose again on our behalf? Jesus tells them plainly: First, they'll live for a divine purpose, and those who believe will display four distinct signs: They'll experience a divine power, they'll enjoy divine communication with Him, they'll have divine protection, and they'll dispense divine healing.

DIVINE PURPOSE

Jesus told them, "Go into all the world and preach the gospel to all creation. Whoever believes and is baptized will be saved, but whoever does not believe will be condemned." At every moment of every day, we have a choice: our will or God's will, our self-seeking agenda or God's self-sacrificing, loving agenda. It's easy to stay in a safe place, but Jesus told them (and us) to break down every barrier and go to any length to tell everyone everywhere about the magnificent gospel of grace.

It's not our job to make anyone believe. That's between each person and God. Like Jesus, we love people enough to go to them and tell them the Good News, and like Him, we never badger or manipulate. We offer His grace, and sometimes we plead with them to turn to Christ and experience His amazing love, but we never twist any arms. We are witnesses, like those who give testimony at a trial. We explain what we have seen and heard, and we let those who are listening decide if they believe our report. Their conclusion doesn't say anything about our testimony or us, but it determines their destiny.

Jesus lists four particular "signs [that] will accompany those who believe."

DIVINE POWER

The first sign is that believers will "drive out demons." This may be strange and scary to many Christians in today's western culture, but not to the disciples who listened to Jesus that day. A few years earlier, He had sent them out two by two with these instructions: "As you go, proclaim this message: 'The kingdom of heaven has come near.' Heal the sick, raise the dead, cleanse those who have leprosy, drive out demons. Freely you have received; freely give" (Matt. 10:7–8).

The vast majority of Christians would say they believe in angels, but they may not understand that demons are fallen angels. Satan, the Enemy, and his legions use four methods to harm people: temptation, deception, accusation, and demonization, which includes oppression, depression, and possession.

- Every person on the planet is tempted to give into lust, greed, prejudice, bitterness, self-pity, and a host of other sins. Temptation isn't sin, but it can lead to sin.

- The Enemy uses deception to make us think that anything on earth—success in our careers, sex, pleasure, or applause—is more valuable than God. Few of the lies we encounter are evident; most of them are either the enticements of advertising or our own desires that seem perfectly reasonable. If we're not careful and sharp, we'll believe what we read, what we hear, and what we feel more than we believe what the Bible says is true about our identity as God's beloved children and our purpose to join Him in changing the world one person at a time.

- Satan is "the accuser of our brothers and sisters" (Rev. 12:10). When we sin, he tries to convince us that we're not forgiven, which makes us cower in fear, wallow in shame, and forget all we've known about God's great grace.

- We read in the gospels and Acts that Jesus cast demons out of people. This occurs when a demon takes residence in a person's body. This still happens today, but in my experience, it seems to occur more in other countries than our own. Oppression is far more common and can become destructive due to its deceptive nature. In every church, and in practically every extended family, people may get saved but still struggle with haunting doubts, addictions, and the effects of past sins and wounds. These create a spiritual bondage that must be broken for the person to thrive.

Jesus was saying, "No matter how the enemy of our souls is putting people in emotional, spiritual, and psychological slavery, I'll set them free!" That's a defining mark of His work in the lives of all believers. It's the new normal for everyone who trusts in Him.

DIVINE COMMUNICATION

Another mark of all those who believe is that they'll enjoy supernatural intimacy with God. In fact, they'll have their own language to connect with God.

Another mark of all those who believe is that they'll enjoy supernatural intimacy with God. In fact, they'll have their own language to connect with God. Jesus said, "They will speak in new tongues." As we pursue God's purpose with God's power, we'll need to stay in close touch with God. In the Old Testament, the Spirit indwelt one person at a time. In the New Testament world, the Spirit resides in all believers, and He gives each of us the ability to hear God's voice and pray in accord with God's supernatural purpose and power. As we pray in tongues, the Spirit prays in us and through us to the Father, according to His perfect will (Rom. 8:26-27).

In Ephesians, Paul explains our divine purpose of representing God in all we do as we "walk in the way of love, just as Christ loved us and gave himself up for us as a fragrant offering and sacrifice to God" (Eph. 5:2). Later in the letter (6:10-20), Paul compares our struggle to fulfill God's purpose with a soldier's love and loyalty for his commander. Every soldier, no matter what his rank, needs to communicate with his superior officer, and all of them get their instructions from the top commander. Prayer is our way of staying connected to our commander, Jesus Christ. Paul reminds us, "And pray in the Spirit on all occasions with all kinds of prayers and requests" (Eph. 6:18). Through Paul, God is telling us to use our prayer language in every conceivable situation—when we're bored and when we're anxious, when things are going well and when the bottom has dropped out, when people speak well of us and when we can't find a friend.

The worldwide mission of evangelism and discipleship can't be accomplished with our own wisdom and strength. We'll become proud when we seem to be making progress, we'll give up in despair when things aren't working out, or more likely, we'll find something else that promises immediate fulfillment without any sacrifice. To be the best soldiers we can be, we simply must get our orders and our power from our only true source: God.

In a battle, soldiers often have plenty of doubts. Sometimes the commands don't make sense, and sometimes the commander's orders demand more than the soldiers think they can do. In the heat of battle, even good soldiers may experience a "lack of faith" and "stubborn refusal to believe" the officer knows what he's doing. In these conditions, good lines of communication are essential—both for a soldier in a regular army and for a soldier in God's army. In every moment, the Spirit of God is in you and with you, praying through you in accord with the perfect will of God. That's the kind of communication we need, and it's exactly what God has provided for us.

Some people claim that the invitation to connect with God by praying "in the Spirit at all times" is past or rare or odd. Jesus said that it's a sign for all who believe. It's present, as common as breathing and as natural as a beloved child communicating with their parent.

DIVINE PROTECTION

Jesus identified another sign of spiritual life for all who believe: "They will pick up snakes with their hands; and when they drink deadly poison, it will not hurt them at all." This may apply to literal places where snakes and poison are encountered (see God's protection of Paul in Acts 28:3-4), but it certainly applies to every space where we feel threatened because we've had the courage to stand up for Christ.

God's purposes take us into dangerous places. He may lead us to a country that has militants who kill Christians, to a land that has infectious diseases, or to backward communities that have almost no modern conveniences. Christ's commission is to "preach the good news to all creation"—no place is off-limits, no people are exceptions.

The most dangerous place for some of us to live and verbalize the gospel isn't the other side of the globe; it's in our own homes, our schools, and our workplaces. Jesus is "the Prince of Peace," but He also warned, "Do not suppose that I have come to bring peace to the earth. I did not come to bring peace, but a sword. For I have come to turn 'a man against his father, a daughter against her mother, a daughter-in-law against her mother-in-law—a man's enemies will be the members of his own household'" (Matt. 10:34–36). If a student walks with spiritual zeal and boldness at school, she may be ostracized by some of her friends. If the fire of God prompts a man to live lovingly, wisely, and boldly for Christ at work, he may lose his job or, at least, be skipped over for promotion. There's always a cost for a life of fire-driven faith.

If you wonder whether faithful, sold-out, servant-minded Christians need protection, ask Paul. At one point, the Corinthians began to wonder if he was the real deal. They saw that he wasn't Superman, so maybe he wasn't such a great apostle after all. Paul's list of credentials could have included his degrees and honors, but instead, he pointed to his sacrifices. He compared his life to the imposters who claimed to represent Christ and attempted to win the allegiance of the Corinthians:

> I have worked much harder, been in prison more frequently, been flogged more severely, and been exposed to death again and again. Five times I received from the Jews the forty lashes minus one. Three times I was beaten with rods, once I was pelted with stones, three times I was shipwrecked, I spent a night and a day in the open sea, I have

been constantly on the move. I have been in danger from rivers, in danger from bandits, in danger from my fellow Jews, in danger from Gentiles; in danger in the city, in danger in the country, in danger at sea; and in danger from false believers. I have labored and toiled and have often gone without sleep; I have known hunger and thirst and have often gone without food; I have been cold and naked. Besides everything else, I face daily the pressure of my concern for all the churches. Who is weak, and I do not feel weak? Who is led into sin, and I do not inwardly burn? (2 Cor. 11:23-29)

In one of his letters to Timothy, Paul shared a truth that must have seemed abundantly self-evident because Timothy had watched his mentor's life very closely: "You, however, know all about my teaching, my way of life, my purpose, faith, patience, love, endurance, persecutions, sufferings—what kinds of things happened to me in Antioch, Iconium and Lystra, the persecutions I endured. Yet the Lord rescued me from all of them. In fact, everyone who wants to live a godly life in Christ Jesus will be persecuted" (2 Tim. 3:10-12). Notice he said "everyone", not some, not even most, but everyone.

When we find ourselves in threatening situations, we don't need to panic and wonder if God has left us high and dry. He hasn't, and He never will. If we're in trouble because we've tried our best to share the love, forgiveness, and power of Christ to people, but we've experienced rejection, we're in good company with Jesus, Paul, Peter, and a host of other believers through the centuries. Divine protection doesn't mean God will make our lives easy; it means the Enemy and the people who follow him can't do anything to us that doesn't pass through God's hands. We may suffer for our faith, but never more than we can bear (see the promise in 1 Cor. 10:13).

If we don't have the fire of the Spirit, we won't be willing to suffer for Christ's sake. We'll opt for enough comfort, enough prestige, and enough success to make our lives acceptable. We won't be *full on* and *full out* for Christ and His kingdom. Our hearts will be guarded, and our obedience will be limited. And if we don't have the fire of God burning in our souls, we won't be praying that God will do miracles to turn Muslims and Hindus and Buddhists to Christ in foreign lands, we won't give sacrificially and gladly to Christ's cause, and we won't be willing to put our children on a plane when they feel called to go to the most dangerous parts of the world. If we don't have divine fire, we won't take risks, so we won't even need divine protection.

God's favor doesn't guarantee that we'll never be in danger, never be criticized, or never be uncomfortable.

God's favor doesn't guarantee that we'll never be in danger, never be criticized, or never be uncomfortable. When we go where God tells us to go, live the way God tells us to live, and speak the words God gives us to say, we're already right in the middle of God's favor. He delights in those who love Him enough to follow Him!

Many of those who heard Jesus that day died martyrs' deaths. God's promise of protection wasn't complete peace and serenity. His promise means that the fire of the Spirit will be with us in our biggest ordeals as we live for Him, and no one . . . *no one* . . . can take us out before the time God has appointed for us. In that, we can rest assured.

DIVINE HEALING

The last of the signs of those who believe is the ability to supernaturally heal people who are sick and hurting: "They will place their hands on sick people, and they will get well." People experience sickness in many different ways: physically, emotionally, mentally, and psychologically. Divine healing can touch each of these problems.

Many people confuse miracles and healing. Miracles happen instantaneously, but healing usually occurs in a process, like the body healing from a broken bone. It doesn't matter how long it takes to heal someone; it only matters that God is active in making it happen.

The laying on of hands is an important part of this process. Touch is powerful. It conveys presence, warmth, and power. Laying on hands isn't some kind of magic. It's God's design for each member of the body of Christ to be involved in one another's lives in a meaningful way. In an article in *Christianity Today*, Nicole Watt summarizes the research findings about the importance of touch: "Research affirms the many benefits of touch. Studies conducted by the Touch Institute in Miami indicate the improvements in sleep and digestion among infants who are massaged regularly. Healthy touch releases endorphins such as the bonding hormone oxytocin and can calm the aggressive behavior of adolescents. Holding hands or giving and receiving hugs on a regular basis can lower blood pressure and calm a racing heartbeat."

James Smith, a counselor at Willow Tree Christian Counseling, observes, "Touch is without a doubt one of the most, if not the most powerful means of communication we have available to us as human beings. We may speak, express ourselves through words, tone, and the volume of our voice, or body language, however nothing comes close to touch."[11]

That's the power of *ordinary* touch. When it is infused with the fire of God and coupled with fervent prayer, the natural healing properties of human touch take on a *divine* dimension.

When we hold someone's hand in the hospital room, when we touch a friend's shoulder, or when we gather with others to pray for someone suffering from a medical condition, addiction, emotional wound, or a haunted past, we then pray to the God whose love and power are beyond anything we can imagine. When we pray in the Spirit with the fire of God directing us, we pray in harmony with the perfect will of God . . . and incredible things happen.

These signs aren't given to us so that we can feel superior to anyone who doesn't have them or to compete with those who do. They aren't measuring sticks of our spirituality or devotion. They are evidences of the power and love of God at work in us and through us. They remind us of the gospel: We were helpless and hopeless in our sin, but Jesus Christ searched for us, found us, paid our penalty, rescued us, and made us His own. With hearts bursting with thankfulness and love, we accept His gifts because they enable us to know Him, love Him, and serve Him even more. The baptism in the Spirit and the expression of tongues accomplish one purpose more than anything else: They enable us to experience even more of Him.

Prayer in the Spirit does not make demands upon God (though our prayers often do), but humbly waits and listens to God—and trusts God the Holy Spirit to intercede for us in keeping God's own will and pleasure.

—Paul Fee

CONSIDER THIS . . .

1. Why is it important to remember that the baptism in the Holy Spirit is a baptism of fire? What happens when we forget this?

2. Read Mark 16:14–18. How does the baptism in the Holy Spirit fit into Christ's commission and promise?

3. Why is it easy to miss God's purpose for the flame, namely, to think it's about the gifts instead of experiencing more of God? What are some practical ways pastors can keep reminding their people of this crucial purpose?

3 THE PATTERN OF THE FLAME

When you strip it of everything else, Pentecost stands for power and life. That's what came into the church when the Holy Spirit came down on the day of Pentecost.

—David Wilkerson

IMAGINE BEING ONE OF THE DISCIPLES THAT DAY IN JERUSALEM at the feast of Pentecost. They hadn't exactly been stellar performers during the years Jesus had been with them! Even after He appeared to them multiple times in resurrection glory, their faith was still weak and wavering. Yet even then, Jesus didn't give up on them. He knew they didn't yet have everything they needed because the Spirit hadn't come to them.

After Jesus told them about the signs that would accompany all who believe, He made good on His promise that He was leaving. Mark tells us the story:

> After the Lord Jesus had spoken to them, he was taken up into heaven and he sat at the right hand of God. Then the disciples went out and preached everywhere, and the Lord worked with them and

confirmed his word by the signs that accompanied it. (Mark 16:19-20)

This isn't just a nice bow on the end of Mark's gospel. Mark wanted to leave Christ's followers with some crucial principles so they could live according to the signs Jesus had just listed. These principles still guide us today:

Get a word from the Lord.

Walking with Christ isn't just a good idea we can take or leave at our convenience. Jesus gave them a word—a summons to follow the King and an invitation to join Him in the family business of redeeming a lost world. Every day, we can get up knowing we have a word from God, a Great Commission given to us by the God of glory, the wise, loving, mighty commander. His Word gives us instructions and all the resources we need to accomplish what He has called us to do.

Jesus has all authority.

After Jesus spoke to them, He ascended and vanished from sight, but He didn't stop existing. "He sat at the right hand of God," the place of ultimate authority where He rules over His divine kingdom through the work of the Spirit.

A few weeks earlier, on the night Jesus was betrayed, He told His men, "Very truly I tell you, whoever believes in me will do the works I have been doing, and they will do even greater things than these, because I am going to the Father. And I will do whatever you ask in my name, so that the Father may be glorified in the Son. You may ask me for anything in my name, and I will do it" (John 14:12-14). The disciples couldn't do "greater things" until Jesus ascended and sent the Holy Spirit on the day of Pentecost. Then, the authority of Christ would be imparted to them—not as a club or a weapon, but as an instrument of justice, righteousness, and kindness, which is exercised in believing prayer and faithful obedience. Praying "in Christ's name" means we're praying in His will and for His glory. When we're praying with fire and love in the Spirit, those criteria are certainly met!

Jesus let us know what is on His heart—the whole world! Thankfully, He has no intention of leaving us to reach and disciple people on our own. We go in His authority, with the fire of the Spirit. Trying to accomplish God's purposes without God's power and authority is like trying to drive a car without gas in the tank. We might push it until we're exhausted, but it won't go far.

Before Jesus ascended, He told His disciples not to push the car until they had gas in the tank: "Do not leave Jerusalem, but wait for the gift my Father promised, which you have heard me speak about. For John baptized with water, but in a few days you will be baptized with the Holy Spirit" (Acts 1:4-5).

Jesus then reiterated the promise and gave them a strategic plan: "But you will receive power when the Holy Spirit comes on you; and you will be my witnesses in Jerusalem, and in all Judea and Samaria, and to the ends of the earth" (Acts 1:8).

They didn't have to wait long for the promise to be fulfilled.

We are Jesus' partners.

Mark tells us that after the Spirit came upon the disciples, "The Lord worked with them." God doesn't bypass us in accomplishing His purposes. He gives us the incredible privilege of being His partners in the greatest enterprise the world has ever known. It's a family business, and we, God's children, delight in getting a word from Him and experiencing His authority and power to fulfill His purposes.

The baptism in the Spirit deepens our experience of divine power, divine communication, divine protection, and divine healing.

The baptism in the Spirit deepens our experience of divine power, divine communication, divine protection, and divine healing. As we move out to do what God's Word has called us to do, we're never alone. He's with us every step of the way.

God gives us powerful reminders.

Mark assures us that God "confirmed his word by the signs that accompanied it" for the first disciples, and He continues to confirm it in our lives today. Only ten days after Jesus vanished into a cloud, the Spirit of God showed up in power and glory on the day of Pentecost. That day, God confirmed His word in many different ways—ways the 120 in the upper room would never forget, and ways they would need to remember later during times of persecution.

The first confirmation happened immediately:

> When the day of Pentecost came, they were all together in one place. Suddenly a sound like the blowing of a violent wind came from heaven and filled the whole house where they were sitting. They saw what seemed to be tongues of fire that separated and came to rest on each of them. All of them were filled with the Holy Spirit and began to speak in other tongues as the Spirit enabled them. (Acts 2:1-4)

For three years, the disciples had watched the power, glory, and love of Jesus. They had seen Him pray all night to the Father, heal the sick, cast out demons, comfort the grieving, teach the crowds, and raise the dead. Near the time of His death, He spent hours explaining what was going to happen when He departed. The Holy Spirit would come upon them, they'd do "greater things," and their prayers would be incredibly powerful. We can imagine they might have been confused, perhaps a bit skeptical—or maybe more than a bit skeptical! They had waited in the upper room for ten days, and the moment had finally arrived. They may have guessed it would be something special, but probably none of them expected anything like this! The sound like a tornado swept through the room and filled the house. A massive ball of fire descended and then split apart, with a flame resting on each person. Suddenly, the promises came true: They were filled with the Holy Spirit and began to speak in tongues! This was the first confirmation, and it gave them courage. Now, they were ready to be the people God had called them to be. Now, they were prepared for the monumental challenge Jesus had put before them.

At some point, the 120 moved to the temple grounds. Pilgrims at the feast had come from all points on the map. When they heard the sound of the mighty wind and the tongues, they were bewildered "because each one heard them speaking in his own language" (Acts 2:6). What were the 120 saying? They weren't telling the pilgrims where they could find a restroom or when the next service started. The disciples were proclaiming the praise of a loving and mighty God and sharing the gospel of grace in languages they'd never learned. The word was going out in Jerusalem!

Some of them were amazed and asked, "What does this mean?" But other pilgrims pushed back. They looked at the miracle in front of their eyes and concluded, "They have had too much wine" (Acts 2:12-13)—as if getting drunk enables people to speak in languages they'd never learned!

The next confirmation was both personal and public. Peter stood up with the Eleven and addressed the crowd. This is the same man who only weeks before had denied he even knew Jesus and the same man who had given up on his part in the mission and had gone fishing because it was the only thing he had confidence he could do. But Jesus didn't give up on Peter. He met him on the shore one morning and assured him of His forgiveness. Now, on the day of Pentecost, the man who had been a coward became a lion. In this moment, Peter didn't rebuke or condemn, and he wasn't defensive. Instead, he was a tender pastor, even to those who accused them of being drunk. He began, "Fellow Jews and all of you who live in Jerusalem, let me explain this to you; listen carefully to what I say. These people are not drunk, as you suppose. It's only nine in the morning" (Acts 2:14-15)!

Peter pointed the people to a passage of Scripture they all had heard before, the prophecy of Joel that God would "pour out [His] Spirit on all people" (Acts 2:17). He quoted David in Psalm 16, and he quoted him again from Psalm 110. Then Peter drew all of his points into one: "Therefore let all Israel be assured of this: God has made this Jesus, whom you crucified, both Lord and Messiah."

The people listening "were cut to the heart" and asked, "Brothers, what shall we do?"

Peter answered with the first three-point invitation in church history: "Repent and be baptized, every one of you, in the name of Jesus Christ for the forgiveness of your sins. And you will receive the gift of the Holy Spirit. The promise is for you and your children and for all who are far off—for all whom the Lord our God will call" (Acts 2:38-39). That day, three thousand people trusted in Christ and were baptized. That was a fantastic confirmation of the promises Jesus had given them!

SIGNS, WONDERS, AND CONFIRMATION

The rest of Luke's account of the early church shows us the pattern of the Holy Spirit's flame in the lives of those who followed Christ. The supernatural signs never stopped, but they often got the disciples in big trouble with the authorities. One day, when Peter and John went to the temple to pray, they saw a beggar who had been crippled from birth. He asked them for money, but they gave him something else: a miracle! He was so thrilled that he jumped for joy. Of course, many people heard what happened, and they came to the temple to see the sight. Peter used this occasion to again tell them about Jesus, but a temple guard and the Sadducees were upset that Peter and John were "proclaiming in Jesus the resurrection of the dead" (Acts 4:2). They arrested the pair, but by this time, the number of new believers had swelled to about five thousand.

The next day, the trial began. Peter and John may have remembered the last time they had seen someone brought before the high priest. It was the first of the mock trials Jesus endured. Peter and John may have assumed their trial would render the same verdict, but they weren't intimidated in the least. They spoke out clearly to share the gospel with the same men who had sentenced Jesus to death. The elders, teachers, and the high priest didn't know how to handle the situation because the crippled man's healing was beyond question. After a private debate, the religious assembly let Peter and John go.

When the two men got back to their group of believers, they told their story, and then "they raised their voices together in prayer to God" (Acts 4:24). Their corporate prayer, voiced by everyone in the room, is beautiful and powerful praise for God's sovereignty over all things. In fact, they remarked that the most tragic event in history was, in God's upside down way of working, His will, the greatest blessing mankind could ever receive. They prayed, "Indeed Herod and Pontius Pilate met together with the Gentiles and the people of Israel in this city to conspire against your holy servant Jesus, whom you anointed. They did what your power and will had decided beforehand should happen" (Acts 4:27-28).

The believers weren't naïve. They fully realized they risked their lives by speaking openly about Jesus, so they trusted God's power more than ever: "Now, Lord, consider their threats and enable your servants to speak your word with great boldness. Stretch out your hand to heal and perform signs and wonders through the name of your holy servant Jesus" (Acts 4:29-30).

Luke tells us how the prayer meeting ended: "After they prayed, the place where they were meeting was shaken. And they were all filled with the Holy Spirit and spoke the word of God boldly" (Acts 4:31).

This was one powerful prayer meeting that ended with the room shaking, the believers filled, and the word continuing to change lives!

When we read Luke's account of this prayer meeting, we're struck by the power, honesty, wisdom, and beauty of their prayer—and that they "raised their voices together" as they prayed this prayer. Perhaps there was a chief spokesman, and they all prayed aloud in agreement, or perhaps they all prayed in the Spirit and Luke recorded the message the Holy Spirit prayed in and through all of those assembled. Either way, this was one powerful prayer meeting that ended with the room shaking, the believers filled, and the word continuing to change lives!

The pattern of divine purpose, power, communication, protection, and healing continues throughout Luke's account in Acts and for the rest of church history. In fact, the existence of over a billion people today who name Christ as their Savior is irrefutable evidence of the "greater things" Jesus has done through those who believe. The power of the Spirit, though, isn't relegated to the elite. God longs to touch and use every believer. In our churches, people often think the pastor is the "hired gun" to do all the important ministry activities. That would have been news to the early Christians. The concept of "the body of Christ" means that everyone plays a critical role, and the body suffers if anyone isn't going full on and full out for Jesus. In Acts 6, an administrative problem led the apostles to appoint some men to organize the food distribution to widows. (Honestly, what could be more mundane than that?) They chose seven men, but the qualifications were high. They had to be "full of the Spirit and wisdom" (Acts 6:3). One of the men chosen was Stephen. This guy wasn't content to sit behind a desk and count boxes of food. Luke tells us about him: "Now Stephen, a man full of God's grace and power, performed great wonders and signs among the people" (Acts 6:8). Some Jewish men opposed him, but they were no match for him because "they could not stand up against the wisdom the Spirit gave him as he spoke" (Acts 6:10).

Stephen's opponents found some unscrupulous men to lie about him, and soon he was arrested and brought before the same tribunal that had tried Jesus and later Peter and John, the Sanhedrin. The accusers lied about him, and then Stephen was allowed to speak. His defense showed how two of the most revered leaders in the Old Testament, Abraham and Moses, pointed to Jesus the Messiah. At the end of his defense, he accused them of being stiff-necked people, with uncircumcised hearts and ears who "resist the Holy Spirit" (Acts 7:51)!

The members of the council were enraged. Stephen knew what was coming. At his moment of peril, he was full of the Spirit. He "looked up to heaven and saw the glory of God, and Jesus standing at the right hand of God. 'Look,' he said, 'I see heaven open and the Son of Man standing at the right hand of God'" (Acts 7:55-56). They dragged him out and stoned him to death.

We might assume that God's promise of protection wasn't fulfilled for Stephen, just as it wasn't for James, who was killed by Herod. We may not know the full reasons for suffering, but we can always be sure that God has a far bigger plan than we can imagine. We get a glimpse of God's mysterious purposes at Stephen's execution. Those who picked up rocks to throw at him needed to take off their outer robes. For safekeeping, they put them at the feet of one of their fiercest defenders, Saul of Tarsus. After this event, Saul went on a rampage, capturing, imprisoning, and killing Christians . . . until Jesus met him on the road to Damascus and changed his life forever. In the years that followed, Saul, now going by his Roman name,

Paul, suffered in every city where he traveled to share the gospel. Who knows how many times he thought of the calm, confident, Holy Spirit-drenched demeanor that enveloped Stephen in his trial and execution? Stephen's death may have given Paul courage in times of persecution when he needed it most.

The message of the gospel and the baptism in the Spirit were always connected, and they still are. When Philip went to Samaria to preach, God worked through him: "When the crowds heard Philip and saw the signs he performed, they all paid close attention to what he said. For with shrieks, impure spirits came out of many, and many who were paralyzed or lame were healed. So there was great joy in that city" (Acts 8:6-8). When reports got back to Jerusalem that people in Samaria—the people the Jews loved to hate—had turned to Christ, the church sent Peter and John to help them grow in their faith. Luke tells us about their ministry there: "When they arrived, they prayed for the new believers there that they might receive the Holy Spirit, because the Holy Spirit had not yet come on any of them; they had simply been baptized in the name of the Lord Jesus. Then Peter and John placed their hands on them, and they received the Holy Spirit" (Acts 8:15-17).

As Jesus instructed and predicted, the gospel spread from Jerusalem to Judea and Samaria. It was about to cross one of the biggest barriers in Jewish tradition: the wall that separated Jews from Gentiles. There was literally a wall in the temple courts that prevented Gentile converts from getting any closer to the temple itself. The barrier, though, wasn't just stone and mortar; it was racial and emotional. God had to work powerfully in Peter's life to help him overcome his deeply entrenched prejudice so he would reach out to Gentiles. God gave him three visions of a sheet containing all kinds of animals, those regularly eaten by Jews and those that were off-limits. God told Peter, "Get up, Peter. Kill and eat" (Acts 10:13).

Suddenly, men appeared at his door. In a vision, the Spirit told Peter that He had sent the men to his house, and he was to go with them. The men took Peter to Caesarea to the home of Cornelius, a Roman centurion who feared God. Cornelius told Peter about the vision God had given him, and Peter realized God was reaching out to embrace people "from every nation" who fear God and do what is right (Acts 10:35). Peter told Cornelius and all those with him about the grace of God through Jesus Christ. Luke explains, "While Peter was still speaking these words, the Holy Spirit came on all who heard the message. The circumcised believers who had come with Peter were astonished that the gift of the Holy Spirit had been poured out even on Gentiles. For they heard them speaking in tongues and praising God" (Acts 10:44-46).

That was enough confirmation for Peter. He announced, "Surely no one can stand in the way of their being baptized with water. They have received the Holy Spirit just as we have" (Acts 10:47).

As Paul traveled to cities to tell people about Christ, he went to Ephesus, a leading city in the Roman Empire and a major port on the west coast of what is now Turkey. He found some disciples there who had only partial understanding of God's truth. Paul asked them, "Did you receive the Holy Spirit when you believed?"

They replied, "No, we have not even heard that there is a Holy Spirit."

Virtually every religious group had their own form of baptism, so Paul asked them what kind of baptism they had received. They told him it was the baptism of John.

Paul explained that John's baptism was the baptism of repentance and they were to look for Jesus, who would come after him. "On hearing this, they were baptized in the name of the Lord Jesus. When Paul placed his hands on them, the Holy Spirit came on them, and they spoke in tongues and prophesied. There were about twelve men in all" (Acts 19:1-7).

These passages demonstrate the clear pattern of the Holy Spirit's work in the lives of the early believers—and He is still at work in the same way today. Speaking in tongues is the initial physical evidence of the baptism in the Spirit, but the main word in this term is "initial." It's not the end; it's only the beginning of a vibrant, thrilling, and challenging relationship with God. The purpose isn't to focus on ourselves, to show off the ability, or to compare ourselves with those around us. The purpose it to experience divine communication with the most powerful, most compassionate, most purposeful Being in the universe . . . nothing less than that.

How little chance the Holy Ghost has nowadays. The churches and missionary societies have so bound Him in red tape that they practically ask Him to sit in a corner while they do the work themselves.

—C. T. Studd

CONSIDER THIS . . .

1. Read Mark 16:19-20. What are some ways you can teach your people the importance of these principles? What difference will it make to them?

2. What are some reasons our people—and we—need God's confirmation with demonstrable signs as we walk with Him?

3. How does the pattern of the baptism in the Spirit and the initial expression of tongues give you confidence to teach this truth to your people?

4 EXAMINING THE FIRE

A church in the land without the Spirit is rather a curse than a blessing. If you have not the Spirit of God, Christian worker, remember that you stand in somebody else's way; you are a fruitless tree standing where a fruitful tree might grow.

—Charles Spurgeon

FROM LUKE'S HISTORICAL ACCOUNT IN ACTS, WE SEE THAT THE baptism in the Spirit, demonstrated by immediately speaking in tongues, was the pattern of spiritual experience in the early church. It was completely normal ... the standard operating procedure.

ANSWERING OBJECTIONS

As we teach about the baptism in the Holy Spirit and the initial physical evidence of tongues, people often ask very good questions. We welcome the opportunity to clarify our positions and help people grow in their faith. We've listed a few of the most common questions they ask.

What about the absence of the baptism in the Spirit and the initial physical evidence of tongues in the New Testament letters?

Some people object that we don't find clear, definitive teaching in the New Testament letters about the baptism in the Spirit and tongues (with the exception of 1 Cor. 12–14). They claim, "For that reason, we can't be dogmatic about the baptism and speaking in tongues." Part of the answer is that we are dogmatic about the Trinity, and yet we have no didactic passages that teach this doctrine. Theologians often use narrative passages like the description of Jesus' baptism to begin to explain the Trinity: Jesus was in the water, "the Spirit of God descended like a dove," and the Father spoke, "This is my Son, whom I love" (Matt. 3:16–17). However, it took church councils hundreds of years to clearly articulate the doctrine of the Trinity, notably in the third century by Origen and Tertullian and later formalized at the Council of Constantinople in 381.

We look at the biblical, historical narrative and the confirmation of church leaders to clarify the teaching about the Trinity. For baptism in the Holy Spirit and tongues, we look at Luke's historical narrative in Acts 2, 10, and 19, and we receive his teaching as sound doctrine. In these three accounts, some details are different, but one common feature is found in all three: When people were baptized in the Holy Spirit, they immediately spoke in tongues. For those who question the use of narrative, we look to Paul's conclusive words to Timothy, "*All Scripture* is God-breathed and is useful for *teaching*, rebuking, correcting and training in righteousness, so that the servant of God may be thoroughly equipped for every good work" (2 Tim. 3:16–17, emphasis ours).

When people are baptized in the Holy Spirit, they can expect to have the same experience we find repeated in Luke's history. They may be in different circumstances, and they may display gifts in addition to tongues, but they can always expect to speak in tongues.

Perhaps there is no mention of the baptism in the Spirit in the New Testament letters because it was the common experience among believers, like breathing is common for all people or being wet is common for fish. No one mentions obvious things unless they're missing or there's a problem, like the problems in Corinth.

What about Paul?

When some people examine Paul's conversion in Acts 9, they conclude that since speaking in tongues isn't mentioned, it didn't happen in his case. Certainly, Luke didn't give us every detail of every event. Similarly, at the end of his gospel, John explains that it's impossible to tell everything. In a sweeping conclusion, he wrote, "Jesus did many other things as well. If every one of them were written down, I suppose that even the whole world would not have room for the books that would be written" (John 21:25). Luke didn't mention tongues in his account of Paul's conversion or subsequent ministry experiences, but we know that Paul spoke in tongues. In fact, he told the tongue-obsessed Corinthians, "I thank God that I speak in tongues more than all of you" (1 Cor. 14:18), and "I would like every one of you to speak in tongues" (1 Cor. 14:5).

How many baptisms are there?

Some of the people who attend our churches are confused about the use of the term *baptism*. It seems to be used in different ways about different experiences. That's exactly right. The Scriptures actually describe three distinct baptisms:

- At the moment of salvation, the Holy Spirit baptizes the new believer into the body of Christ. Paul wrote, "For we were all baptized by one Spirit so as to form one body—whether Jews or Gentiles, slave or free— and we were all given the one Spirit to drink" (1 Cor. 12:13).

- A new believer is baptized in water by another Christian. We see descriptions of this in many places in the New Testament, including the accounts of the three thousand who believed when Peter preached at Pentecost (Acts 2), the Samaritans who were converted when Philip preached to them (Acts 8), the Ethiopian eunuch (Acts 8), Paul (Acts 9), Cornelius (Acts 10), Lydia and her family (Acts 16), the Philippian jailer and his family (Acts 16), and Crispus and his household (Acts 18).

- Believers are baptized by Jesus in the Holy Spirit. John the Baptist explains that Jesus would "baptize you in the Holy Spirit and fire" (Luke 3:16; see also Matt. 3:11, Mark 1:8, and John 1:33).

All three are crucial. When people are touched by the gospel of grace and turn to Christ, the Holy Spirit baptizes them into the body of Christ, and all the blessings of adoption become theirs. Water baptism is a public testimony of the new birth so that everyone will know a new life has begun. To be a public witness and live sacrificially and joyfully for Christ in a fallen world, they need to be baptized in the Holy Spirit and fire. Nothing less provides the light and power necessary to represent Christ to a dying world—on the other side of the planet or on the other side of the house.

To be a public witness and live sacrificially and joyfully for Christ in a fallen world, they need to be baptized in the Holy Spirit and fire.

What is "the second work of grace"?

Some people who hear the teaching about the baptism in the Holy Spirit are perplexed for a different reason. They thought they already had the Spirit, and they assume we're teaching they don't have the Spirit . . . which seems to invalidate their spiritual experiences.

Traditional Pentecostal teaching is that at the moment of salvation, the Holy Spirit baptizes the new believer into the body of Christ, assures the person of forgiveness, and confirms a new position as a son or daughter of God. The Spirit dwells in the new believer from the moment of conversion (1 Cor. 6:19–20). A second work of grace, usually at a later date, is the baptism in the Spirit.

After Jesus was raised from the dead, He met often with His disciples. At the end of the first week after He first appeared, the disciples were hiding. The Jewish leaders had killed Jesus, and they were sure they were next on the list. In their hideout, Jesus came to them. He said, "Peace be with you!" To assure them again that He wasn't a ghost or the product of their fear-hyped imaginations, He showed them the holes in His hands and His side. They must have been really scared because He told them again, "Peace be with you!" This time, He gave them the Great Commission: "As the Father has sent me, I am sending you." Then He breathed on them and said, "Receive the Holy Spirit" (John 20:19–22).

This was the moment of their conversion. It reminded John's first readers of the Genesis story when God breathed life into Adam (Gen. 2:7). Before His ascension, Jesus told them to wait in Jerusalem for the gift the Father promised, which is the baptism in the Holy Spirit (Acts 1:4–5). A few days later, the disciples were baptized in the Spirit on the day of Pentecost when the sound of rushing winds filled the room and tongues of fire touched each one.

In Acts 8, Philip preached in Samaria, and many "accepted the word of the Lord." When the leaders in Jerusalem heard this news, they "sent Peter and John to Samaria. When they arrived, they prayed for the new believers there that they might receive the Holy Spirit, because the Holy Spirit had not yet come on any of them; they had simply been baptized in the name of the Lord Jesus. Then Peter and John placed their hands on them, and they received the Holy Spirit" (Acts 8:14–17).

Luke describes some accounts of people being baptized in the Spirit as soon as they believed. This happened to Cornelius and the people who were with him (Acts 10).

In Acts 19, Paul met "some disciples" who had "believed," but they only had a partial understanding of the gospel. When Paul explained the full message of Jesus' death and resurrection, "they were baptized into the name of Jesus." When Paul laid hands on them, "the Holy Spirit came on them, and they spoke in tongues and prophesied" (Acts 19:1–7). Simultaneous conversion and baptism in the Holy Spirit happened occasionally, but it is an exception to the general pattern found in Acts.

How does the baptism in the Spirit relate to the filling of the Spirit?

Many church leaders equate the baptism in the Spirit with the filling of the Spirit. Certainly, when we are baptized in the Spirit, He fills us. The initial experience of Spirit baptism, though, is only the beginning of a life of intimacy and power in a relationship with God. In his letter to the Ephesians, Paul draws the contrast: "Do not get drunk on wine, which leads to debauchery. Instead, be filled with the Spirit" (Eph. 5:18). Alcohol dulls the mind and distorts a person's judgment, but the Spirit of God has the opposite effect: Being filled with the Spirit leads to wisdom (vv. 15–17), joyful hearts, gratitude, obedience, and humility (vv. 19–21). The Greek verb in verse 18 is a present imperative. It doesn't describe a one-time event, but an ongoing connection to the Spirit of God: It means "keep on being filled with the Spirit."

Similarly, Paul wrote to the Galatians to encourage them to "keep in step with the Spirit" (Gal. 5:25). The context of this directive was the moment by moment choice to "walk in the Spirit" and not "gratify the desires of the flesh." Paul illustrates the inner conflict all Christians face between our sinful desires and God's perfect will, between our selfish agendas and God's kingdom agenda for us. He contrasts the "acts of the flesh" (Gal. 5:19–21) with the "fruit of the Spirit" (Gal. 5:22–23). The choice to keep in step with the Spirit is often a difficult one that requires spiritual courage. To encourage them (and us) to make good choices, Paul reminds them of their past choice to follow Jesus: "Those who belong to Christ Jesus have crucified the flesh with its passions and desires" (Gal. 5:24). So, a Spirit-filled life is one that begins with the baptism in the Spirit and continues to deepen and grow as we keep in step with Him.

Is the baptism in the Spirit still for today?

In the Mark 16 passage, we saw that Jesus said tongues would be a sign to those who believe in Him. He told the disciples to wait in Jerusalem for "the gift my Father promised. . . . For John baptized with water, but in a few days you will be baptized with the Holy Spirit" (Acts 1:4–5). And John the Baptist explained that Jesus will "baptize you with the Holy Spirit and fire" (Luke 3:16). In *Fresh Wind, Fresh Fire*, pastor and author Jim Cymbala notes:

> Some have said, "The miracles, signs, and wonders of the book of Acts were temporary. They served to authenticate the apostles until such time as the New Testament could be written. Now we have the completed Word of God, which erases the need for supernatural happenings." My response is this: If we have a completed revelation in written

form, are we seeing at least as much advance for
God's kingdom, as many people coming to Christ,
as many victories over Satan as those poor fellows
who had to get along with just the Old Testament?
If not, why not? Are we missing something valuable that they felt was essential?[12]

If Jesus promised the baptism in the Spirit, performs
it in us, and then uses it to give us divine purpose, power,
communication, protection, and healing, why in the world
wouldn't we receive that baptism with hearts overflowing
with gratitude?

Of course, we're thoroughly human, and we mess
things up. Like all good gifts God hands us, we can let our
selfishness and foolishness turn them into something less
than God intends. It's the same with the manifestation of
the Spirit in tongues. We can shake our heads at the immaturity of the Corinthians and their trouble with tongues,
but because they struggled and failed, we have Paul's clear
teaching about how to use this gift in public and private.

GIFTS AND LOVE

Corinth was a thriving port in the Roman Empire. Ships
arrived from all over the Mediterranean. It was only a short
haul across the isthmus as a shortcut to Athens, Ephesus,
and Palestine. Busy ports are exciting places to live and
visit—full of entrepreneurs, prostitutes, sailors, and wealth,
and Corinth was a crossroads of culture, money, and power.
It's not surprising, then, that the church in the city had problems with pride, selfishness, stinginess, superiority, and all
other forms of immaturity and arrogance. Paul's first letter

to the believers in Corinth is a litany of corrections. In most of his letters, he affirms Christians for their faith and faithfulness. His letter to the Corinthians is different. After a few introductory comments of gratitude, Paul launches into his list of important issues: divisions, factions, and bitterness; intellectual arrogance; ignoring spiritual authority; gross immorality—and failure to address the problem; lawsuits that happen because brothers and sisters in Christ can't find a solution to their disagreements; rampant sexual sins; failure to honor marriage; insisting on personal rights at others' expense; suspicion of Paul's role as their leader; and blaspheming the Lord's Supper. (How would you like to be the pastor of that church?) In light of all these misconceptions and sinful passions, it's no wonder they didn't understand the role of spiritual gifts.

In three chapters, Paul spells out the identity, nature, and practice of the gifts, and particularly, the ones that are often called "sign gifts." He lists them in Chapter 12. We might categorize them in three groups of three:

- Revelatory gifts
    Words of wisdom
    Words of knowledge
    Discerning of spirits
- Vocal gifts
    Prophecy
    Speaking in tongues
    Interpretation of tongues
- Power gifts
    Faith
    Healing
    Working of miracles

Paul doesn't go into a long explanation about how to use each of these gifts—not yet at least. He only identifies their source: "All these are the work of one and the same Spirit, and he distributes them to each one, just as he determines" (1 Cor. 12:11).

Every person, no matter how exalted or humble, plays a crucial role in the vitality of a church, and in fact, the most humble servants are, in Paul's estimation, the most important.

One of the chief problems in the Corinthian church was a lack of unity. The people—and, it seems, the leaders, too—jockeyed for positions of power and prestige. Paul used the metaphor of the human body to show how power plays are self-destructive. He didn't use only a verse or two to make his point. Unity (we can assume from the length and depth of his description) is essential if a church is to use the gifts properly. Every person, no matter how exalted or humble, plays a crucial role in the vitality of a church, and in fact, the most humble servants are, in Paul's estimation, the most important. He explains, "But God has put the body together, giving greater honor to the parts that lacked it, so that there should be no division in the body, but that its parts should have equal concern for each other. If one part suffers, every part suffers with it; if one part is honored, every part rejoices with it" (1 Cor. 12:24-26).

Paul then reiterates the list of the gifts and concludes that none is above another, but one thing is supremely important: love. It is, he asserts, "the most excellent way" (1 Cor. 12:31).

We often hear 1 Corinthians 13 read at weddings, and the people usually sigh and smile. They don't have a clue what Paul is saying! He is giving the Corinthians a stinging rebuke. In a few short verses, he confronts their arrogance, foolishness, immaturity, and superiority.

First, without love, tongues mean nothing—they are like the noise of pagan priests banging cymbals in their temples: "If I speak in the tongues of men or of angels, but do not have love, I am only a resounding gong or a clanging cymbal" (v. 1).

Then, Paul corrects their assumption that prophetic gifts, words of wisdom and knowledge, and supernatural, visionary faith give them status over others: "If I have the gift of prophecy and can fathom all mysteries and all knowledge, and if I have a faith that can move mountains, but do not have love, I am nothing" (v. 2).

And finally, Paul rebukes their pride in "all they've sacrificed for Jesus"—and it wasn't just money; Paul says that if actions aren't driven by genuine love, even the ultimate sacrifice of our lives is totally worthless: "If I give all I possess to the poor and give over my body to hardship that I may boast, but do not have love, I gain nothing" (v. 3).

Nothing ... empty ... worthless. Even the most dramatic expressions of spiritual gifts have no value if they aren't inspired, directed, and empowered by authentic love.

Paul then gives a list of words describing this kind of love, but again, this is a thinly veiled rebuke. Earlier in the letter, Paul had chastened the Corinthians for their lack of patience, lack of kindness, envy and boasting, rudeness, self-promotion, anger, resentment, amusement of evil, and failure to protect innocent people. People at weddings may sigh when this passage is read, but the people in Corinth undoubtedly cringed!

As a wise and loving pastor, Paul also reminded them of a person who perfectly exemplifies the characteristics of genuine love. Jesus is perfectly patient, self-sacrificing, kind, forgiving, and protecting. He delights in love, justice, and truth, and His love never fails.

It's easy, Paul implies, for us to fix our eyes on the dramatic gifts and miss the heart of Jesus. But that's not all. It's also easy for us to focus on today and miss the ultimate promise of a glorious tomorrow. There will come a day when we don't need the sign gifts any longer. On that day, our divine communication will be up close and personal:

> Love never fails. But where there are prophecies, they will cease; where there are tongues, they will be stilled; where there is knowledge, it will pass away. For we know in part and we prophesy in part, but when completeness comes, what is in part disappears. When I was a child, I talked like a child, I thought like a child, I reasoned like a child. When I became a man, I put the ways of childhood behind me. For now we see only a reflection as in a mirror; then we shall see face to face. Now I know in part; then I shall know fully, even as I am fully known. (1 Cor. 13:8–12)

Before that day, we still have plenty of work to do on our attitudes and relationships. We get off track so easily! Many things seem important, but only one is of supreme value. Paul concludes, "And now these three remain: faith, hope and love. But the greatest of these is love" (1 Cor. 13:13).

All the gifts have been imparted to us so that we can fulfill the Great Commandment to love God with all our hearts and love our neighbor as ourselves. If the gifts have any other impact on us and our love for the least and the lost, we've missed it. We've badly missed it.

The Spirit's work isn't about being self-indulgent or having a goose-bumped emotional experience with God.

The Spirit's work isn't about being self-indulgent or having a goose-bumped emotional experience with God. In his book, *Toward Pentecostal Unity*, Donald Gee encourages church leaders to trust God for a powerful, life-changing blend of the Spirit's work. He explains, "We ought not enjoy deep emotion at the expense of shallow thinking. 'I will pray with the spirit but I will pray with the understanding also' is the scriptural way of putting it. The three golden strands of order, faith, and experience need weaving into the one cord that cannot quickly be broken. A Pentecostal revival in the fullest measure will not stress one at the expense of the others but will manifest a shining witness to all three."[13]

THE PRACTICE

In the next chapter in his letter to the Christians in Corinth, Paul provides clear guidelines about the use of tongues, but first, he repeats the importance of love and the preeminence of prophetic words: "Follow the way of love and eagerly desire gifts of the Spirit, especially prophecy" (1 Cor. 14:1). Tongues are both the initial public evidence and an integral part of private and public worship, but prophecy and teaching are more important in church services. Paul explains, "Now, brothers and sisters, if I come to you and speak in tongues, what good will I be to you, unless I bring you some revelation or knowledge or prophecy or word of instruction?" (v. 6)

Speaking in tongues, Paul explains, engages our spirits and bypasses our minds (v. 14). We are able to pray without any interference from our souls, our natural desires and attitudes, so our prayers are in accordance with the Spirit of God and the Father's will. This kind of prayer enables us to be completely submitted to God. The tongue and the brain are integrally connected. James tells us that the tongue has great power—for good or ill, to praise God or curse people (James 3:1-12). When we pray in tongues, our spirits connect with the Spirit and submit to the will and ways of God.

One of the criticisms—too often, accurate criticisms— of Spirit-filled churches is that they exercise the gifts in a way that manipulates people, induces guilt motivation to control them, and exalts some people over others. These are evidences of the flesh, not the Spirit. They are exactly the problems Paul so carefully addressed in his letter to the Corinthians.

In his correction for the church, Paul provides clear teaching and practical guidelines. The Corinthians were, we can surmise, having tongue-talking contests. They were trying to impress each other with the fervor, length, or some other feature of the expression of tongues. Paul explains that it's not about impressing anyone; it's about connecting with God: "For anyone who speaks in a tongue does not speak to people but to God. Indeed, no one understands them; they utter mysteries by the Spirit" (1 Cor. 14:2). This is the essence of an intimate connection: God is speaking in us and through us back to Himself. This divine communication is, then, completely in agreement with God's divine purposes, so it gives added boldness and confidence to John's promise: "This is the confidence we have in approaching God: that if we ask anything according to his will, he hears us. And if we know that he hears us—whatever we ask—we know that we have what we asked of him" (1 John 5:14-15).

This confidence doesn't mean we don't experience tension as we pray. As our hearts are in alignment with God, He often exposes our selfish desires—even those that have been hidden for a long time. When Jesus prayed in the Garden before His arrest, He asked, "Abba, Father, . . . everything is possible for you. Take this cup from me." When He looked into the abyss of bearing the sin of the entire world, He recoiled from the prospect of infinite suffering and separation from the Father—but His prayer wasn't finished. He concluded, "Yet not what I will, but what you will"

(Mark 14:36). Tension? Yes, Jesus felt enormous tension as He prayed. We'll never suffer the same level of inner conflict, but we'll certainly experience a fair share when our natural desire collides with God's good and perfect will, which inevitably involves turning our world upside down so that we pursue His heart, His desires, and His kingdom more than our own selfish agendas.

In this part of his letter, Paul isn't focused only on tongues, although it is apparent that the Corinthians' main problem was with that gift. Paul widens the perspective by explaining: "Anyone who speaks in a tongue edifies themselves, but the one who prophesies edifies the church. I would like every one of you to speak in tongues, but I would rather have you prophesy. The one who prophesies is greater than the one who speaks in tongues, unless someone interprets, so that the church may be edified" (1 Cor. 14:4–5).

Paul makes the observation that personal edification is certainly a benefit, but for an expression of tongues to benefit others, an interpretation must be given: "For this reason the one who speaks in a tongue should pray that they may interpret what they say" (v. 13). He continues with his reasoning for this instruction. He shares that he wants everyone to benefit from the message of tongues, not just the speaker:

> For if I pray in a tongue, my spirit prays, but my mind is unfruitful. So what shall I do? I will pray with my spirit, but I will also pray with my understanding; I will sing with my spirit, but I will also sing with my understanding. Otherwise when you

are praising God in the Spirit, how can someone
else, who is now put in the position of an inquirer,
say "Amen" to your thanksgiving, since they do not
know what you are saying? You are giving thanks
well enough, but no one else is edified. (1 Cor.
14:14-17)

Many pastors and church leaders—including the two
of us for many years—have overlooked the principle of
praying for the interpretation. Paul clearly instructs those
who speak in tongues to also pray for the interpretation.
This applies to both public and private expressions. We
might explain his logic this way: When we pray in tongues,
our minds are unfruitful, and others don't know what
we're saying. The speaker is edified, but others are left
in the dark. Paul's solution is for the person speaking to
also pray that God will give an interpretation to them or
to someone who operates in the gift of interpretation of
tongues so that everyone will benefit. If we're praying in
tongues in a small group, we can ask God for an interpretation, and then wait for it. In our personal times of praying
in the Spirit, we can also ask God for the interpretation of
our prayers. If we wait and expect Him to give it, He will.

No matter where we are, we can follow Paul's example:
"I will pray with my spirit, but I will also pray with my
understanding; I will sing with my spirit, but I will also sing
with my understanding" (v. 15). With the interpretation, we
can bring our flesh into submission with our spirit. Again,
we may experience tension, but that's entirely good, right,
and normal. It's part of the struggle for still flawed but
redeemed people to walk with God in this life.

The staff, board, and elders at our churches have been taught and trained to ask God for an interpretation. When we start meetings, we take time to pray in the Spirit. When everyone is finished, we ask, "Has God said anything to you?" Quite often, someone has a word from the Lord that applies to our task at hand or to our team.

In our private times of prayer in the Spirit, early in the morning or at any time of the day, we ask, "Lord, are You telling me something through my prayers?" Quite often, He gives a word of encouragement, correction, or instruction. Very often, these times of prayer are quite fluid. We might pray in the Spirit, listen for an interpretation, pray in our native tongue, sing in the Spirit, and then sing in our native tongue . . . or some other order.

Paul makes sure the Corinthians understand that he values his experience of tongues. He assures them, "I thank God that I speak in tongues more than all of you" (1 Cor. 14:18). Was this just preacher hyperbole? Probably not. No one faced more stress, persecution, and opposition than Paul. If anyone needs to be intimately connected to God and benefit from divine communication, it's those who are suffering for their faith. Paul was strengthened so that he could keep leading, preaching, and representing Christ— even to those who wanted to kill him.

If you're not going to be a witness for Christ, you may not need the baptism in the Spirit. If you don't need power to take you to places you've never been, maybe you don't need the fire. The 120 at Pentecost and the rest of the believers in the book of Acts desperately needed the fullness of the Spirit because the task God had given them was far bigger than they could accomplish by themselves. Is our task any smaller? Is our mission field any safer? Do the people who need Christ today have less need for the Spirit of God to convict them of sin, righteousness, and judgment? Do we need the supernatural presence and power of God less today than they did in the first century?

Paul couldn't live without an intimate, divine connection. He wanted to be in direct communication with the Spirit of God at all times and in all places.

This part of Paul's letter to the Corinthians is part correction, part instruction, and part encouragement. The Christians in that church had made a mess of the use of the gifts. Paul corrects and teaches them about the intended audience for the gift of tongues in church services. It is a sign, he explains, "not for believers but for unbelievers; prophecy, however, is not for unbelievers but for believers" (1 Cor. 14:22). Like our churches today, a service often had both Christians and unbelievers in attendance. God wanted to speak to both. Tongues and the interpretation were to give the message of the gospel to those who needed to be saved—just as tongues were used at Pentecost in Jerusalem to speak to the pilgrims from all over the Roman world.

God may use prophecy in the lives of both believers and unbelievers. Paul explains, "But if an unbeliever or an inquirer comes in while everyone is prophesying, they are convicted of sin and are brought under judgment by all, as the secrets of their hearts are laid bare. So they will fall down and worship God, exclaiming, 'God is really among you'" (1 Cor. 14:24-25)!

Paul ends his teaching about the use of the gifts by pre-scribing order for the services. Two people, or at the most three, should speak in tongues, but only after each one is interpreted. If there is no interpretation, the person should stay quiet. In the same way, two or three people should give words of prophecy, but only in turn and with time for people to "weigh carefully" what has been said. Paul did not include the restrictive clause, "at the most" regarding the gift of prophecy.

Order, Paul insists, isn't a limitation on the use of the gifts. Instead, it frees people to flow in the gifts so that God can use them to accomplish great things. He concludes, "But everything should be done in a fitting and orderly way" (1 Cor. 14:40).[14]

If you're a pastor, most of the biblical principles in this chapter aren't new or foreign, but in our experience, these concepts are fresh and inspiring to many of the people who come to our churches.

The fullness of the Holy Spirit gives us great comfort, but often only after He shakes us to the core. Old assump-tions are shattered, and the secret idols of adulation and prestige are surfaced and slain. Evangelist and revivalist R. A. Torrey has observed that many pastors pray for the baptism in the Spirit and the rushing wind of revival, but in reality, they actually want growth and fame, not purging and fire. He shares the following insight:

Many a church is praying for a revival that does not really desire a revival. They think they do, for to their minds a revival means an increase of membership, an increase of income, an increase of reputation among the churches; but if they knew what a real revival meant, what a searching of hearts on the part of professed Christians would be involved, what a radical transformation of individual, domestic and social life would be brought about, and many other things that would come to pass if the Spirit of God was poured out in reality and power; if all this were known the real cry of the church would be: "O God, keep us from having a revival."

Many a minister is praying for the filling with the Holy Spirit who does not really desire it. He thinks he does, for the filling with the Spirit means to him new joy, new power in preaching the Word, a wider reputation among men, a larger prominence in the church of Christ. But if he understood what a filling with the Holy Spirit really involved, how for example it would necessarily bring him into antagonism with the world and with unspiritual Christians, how it would cause his name to be "cast out as evil," how it might necessitate his leaving a good comfortable living and going down to work in the slums, or even in some foreign land; if he understood all this, his prayer quite likely would be—if he were to express the real wish of his heart—"O God, save me from being filled with the Holy Ghost."[15]

Lord, give us a longing for nothing less than your fire—whatever it may cost!

> For Paul . . . the Spirit is none other than the fulfillment of the promise that God Himself would once again be present with His people.
>
> —Gordon D. Fee

CONSIDER THIS . . .

1. Which of the questions in the beginning section of this chapter have you been asked most often? Which ones do you feel most confident to answer? How can you help others in your church provide good answers to their friends?

2. In what ways is your church like the Corinthians? How is it different? Which of Paul's corrections would be helpful in your church?

3. How does it (or would it) affect your praying in the Spirit to ask God for an interpretation and listen for His answer?

5 THE FIRE ON SUNDAY MORNING

May God so fill us today with the heart of Christ that we may glow with the divine fire of holy desire.

—A. B. Simpson

TODAY, WE ENJOY THE EFFECTS OF COMBUSTION IN COUNTLESS ways, but the reality of fire is usually hidden under the hoods of our cars, in the attic encased in our furnaces, or converted to heating elements on the stove or the oven. Still, we have some exposure to genuine flames in the fireplace in winter (even if we use gas logs), our propane or charcoal grills, or a back patio *chiminea*. All of these are contained, controlled, and occasional. We live in a microwave society. Heat is generated quickly and conveniently without any of the messiness of wood or coal stoves that our grandparents used only a few generations ago.

In the spiritual world, it's easy to mistake enthusiasm or loudness for the fire of the Holy Spirit. Years ago, the founder of the Salvation Army, William Booth, warned, "There are different kinds of fire; there is false fire. No one knows this better than we do, but we are not such fools as to refuse good bank notes because there are false ones in circulation; and although we see here and there manifestations of what appears to us to be nothing more than mere earthly fire, we none the less prize and value, and seek for the genuine fire which comes from the altar of the Lord."[16]

As we've described, church services on Sunday nights in earlier generations didn't resemble a microwave culture. People "tarried," waiting on the Lord to bring the fire of the Holy Spirit in His timing. They expected a long service, so no one was anxious when it wasn't over at a specified time. Many families planned on a full evening on Sunday nights. In fact, they expected to be tired by the end of it. The whole family attended the evangelistic preaching, the altar call, and the expression of gifts, including people being baptized in the Spirit. Children got tired and slept on the pews (or under the pews). After the long service finally ended, the families often went out to eat to talk about what the Lord had done in people's lives. By the time they got home, the children were exhausted, but everyone had a sense that God had done something wonderful in the lives of people at the service.

Today, most people aren't willing to devote themselves to a seemingly endless meeting. They are more rigidly scheduled. Television shows last thirty minutes, an hour, or at most, two hours. This pattern has shaped the expectations of our culture. We block out a certain amount of time for any event in church, and people expect it to be over at the appointed time. They have other things to do: programs to watch, books to read, children to put in bed, or internet sites to view. If church activities last any longer than an hour (or at most an hour and a half), people wonder if it's worth coming back again. We should not and cannot change our theology, but we have to find a way to be both biblically astute and culturally relevant.

The timing and the schedule of our meetings have to fit the culture, but the fire isn't optional . . . and the fire always starts with the leader.

THE TORCH

> There's little or no heat in a church if the leader isn't flaming. The pastor has to have a genuine, consecrated, ongoing, vibrant connection with God.

There's little or no heat in a church if the leader isn't flaming. The pastor has to have a genuine, consecrated, ongoing, vibrant connection with God. The grace of God isn't something we experience at salvation and then we just try very hard for the rest of our lives. The beauty and power of the gospel needs to be a source of continual wonder, and the reality of the Spirit is a constant source of fire to keep the pastor's passion hot—not simmering, not warm, but *hot*. It's easy to let our fire fade to a flicker. Paul warned the Corinthians, "But I am afraid that just as Eve was deceived by the serpent's cunning, your minds may somehow be led astray from your sincere and pure devotion to Christ" (2 Cor. 11:3). Right doctrine isn't enough. Pastors need to practice what they say they believe. In his earlier letter, Paul said that praying in the Spirit wasn't optional for him: "I thank God that I speak in tongues more than all of you" (1 Cor. 14:18).

Paul's statement probably served two purposes. First, he assured them that he wasn't against tongues at all. His letter was corrective—of their motives and their public practice. It appears they were out of control in their expression of tongues, and Paul reined them in. But he didn't want them to misunderstand. He wasn't against tongues, only against the misuse of the gift. He wanted to confirm that the gift of tongues plays a vital role in the life of the body of Christ. Second, Paul told them that he spoke in the Spirit more than anyone else because he wanted to be intimately connected to the power, love, and wisdom of God as he experienced the pressures of leadership and the suffering of persecution. Praying in the Spirit enabled him to bypass his mind and his understanding so he could tap directly into the Spirit of God. He realized that he needed to hear from God.

It appears that Paul didn't realize he was writing Scripture when he wrote letters to the churches and his friends Timothy, Titus, and Philemon. He was the human author, but he needed to be perfectly in tune with the divine author, the Holy Spirit. If he didn't pray in the Spirit "more than any" other people, he may not have had the wisdom and insight to write words God still uses to teach, rebuke, correct, and train believers in righteousness on every continent and in every culture until Christ returns.

Paul is an example for all pastors. All of us experience crushing responsibilities. Shepherding God's people and reaching the lost is exhausting . . . and often, confusing.

Like Paul, we need to hear from God, so it would be logical for us to pray in the Spirit more than any of our people so that we are equipped and empowered to lead them.

Some people mistakenly believe that praying in the Spirit makes us feel invincible. The reality is quite the opposite . . . for Paul and for us. Near the end of his life, Paul called himself "the worst" of sinners (1 Tim. 1:15). Some might assume he was referring to his past before he met Jesus on the road to Damascus. He had been a kidnapper and murderer. However, the verb tense in his letter to Timothy is present: "I am the worst." This wasn't some kind of self-hatred or the symptom of a psychological disorder. Since the day he had met Christ decades earlier, Paul got closer to God and experienced more of His love and grace. With a deeper grasp of the wonder of God's acceptance, he could be more honest about the sins and flaws in his life.

Similarly, when Paul experienced suffering from his "thorn in the flesh," he naturally asked God for healing and relief. Instead, God gave him assurance that the suffering had a higher purpose: "My grace is sufficient for you, for my power is made perfect in weakness." Paul responded with humble, grateful, openhanded faith: "Therefore I will boast all the more gladly about my weaknesses, so that Christ's power may rest on me. That is why, for Christ's sake, I delight in weaknesses, in insults, in hardships, in persecutions, in difficulties. For when I am weak, then I am strong" (2 Cor. 12:9-10).

Far from making us feel invincible, praying in the Spirit and walking close to God give us humility to confess our sins because we're assured of His forgiveness, and they

give us courage to admit we're weak because we're convinced God will be strong on our behalf.

Instead of ignoring, minimizing, or denying our sins
and weaknesses, we can embrace them because the glory
of God is best shown in cracked pots (2 Cor. 4:7f). If we'll
be honest with God about our flaws, we'll enjoy more of
His tenderness, His assurance, and His power than ever
before. Humility is the kindling for the fire of God in our
lives. We say, "Lord, it's not about me. It's all about You. I'm
completely Yours. Use me in any way that brings You glory."
When we're serving to win approval, or when we think
we know how to make ministry work, we use God for our
purposes instead of being open to serve the rightful King.
But when we live and love in humility and dependence,
God inevitably sends the fire.

IGNITING OTHERS

**Kingdom life only makes sense if we
begin with the One who lived in
splendor but gave it all up to live and
die for sinners.**

When pastors and church leaders experience the fire
of the Spirit, they want everyone they know to experience
more of God, too. Like us, our people resist being honest
about their sins and weaknesses. Our culture is based on

image management, impressing people in any and every way possible, but life in the Spirit is countercultural and upside down. Kingdom life only makes sense if we begin with the One who lived in splendor but gave it all up to live and die for sinners, One who became the lowest servant out of love, and One who lost His reputation so we could be accepted and made coheirs forever.

When we experience the fire, we want our torch to touch our spouse and children, our board and top leaders, all the others who serve at our church, the entire congregation, our communities, and the world. The fire expands from a single flame to ignite people in a widening circle— to as many as are open to the touch of the Spirit.

If we're not igniting people around us, there could be one of two problems: Either they are damp wood and refuse to light, or we aren't really on fire. A genuine fire can't be easily contained. By its nature, it consumes fuel, spreads, and grows. Spiritually, a true fire can't be contained either. When Jeremiah tried to block the fire of the Spirit in his life, he realized it was useless. He remarked, "But if I say, 'I will not mention his word or speak anymore in his name,' his word is in my heart like a fire, a fire shut up in my bones. I am weary of holding it in; indeed, I cannot" (Jer. 20:9). There is no such thing as a "closet Charismatic." If the Spirit is real to us, we'll find a way to share the experience of God's fire with others. If we're not gladly and spontaneously talking about the wonder of God, sensing the face of God, hearing the voice of God, and finding the love of God, there's probably very little fire in our own hearts.

Let's be clear: We're not talking about promoting a particular experience or a church or a pastor. That's not what the fire is about. We're talking about tapping into the only true source of love, power, and wisdom that transforms people's lives. We want everyone to have a vital, genuine experience of the very presence of Almighty God! Then arrogant people become humble, fearful people find courage, outcasts are brought in, prejudiced people warmly accept others, fools become wise, the weak become strong, and grouches are thankful.

A NEW MATCH

My (John's) great-grandmother went to a traditional Methodist church in a small, Texas town in the '30s. In those days, people wore their best clothes to her church. It had stained glass windows and a choir with robes. A friend invited her to go to a storefront Pentecostal church with crude benches and sawdust on the floor. It was a stereotype of the new Pentecostal movement. The experience of worship, though, was fiery. People sang loudly (and perhaps off key), the preacher spoke with zeal, and the gifts were freely expressed. People sometimes yelled, "Hallelujah!" When people were overcome with the presence and power of God, they might run or jump over the benches. During the prayer time when hands were laid on people, they sometimes fell on the sawdust floor and rolled around. When I was a boy, she told me, "Son, I really saw holy rollers!"

My great-grandmother was shocked by all of this, but she was intrigued because she sensed these people had something in their relationship with God that she lacked. She saw genuine miracles of healing. They were people she knew, so no one could dispute the work of God in their bodies and their lives. One Sunday during an altar call, she went down and accepted Christ. She had been a faithful church member before that day, but she hadn't been born again. Sometime later, she was baptized in the Holy Spirit and spoke in tongues. One by one, the rest of her family came to Christ.

That was over eight decades ago. Today, if my great-grandmother were a young woman who was a member of a mainline denomination and was invited to a Pentecostal church, would she notice any difference? Would she see the fire? Would she recognize the genuineness of the people's faith? Would she be drawn to Christ because of the irrefutable work of the Spirit? Those are questions we are wise to consider.

Today, the vast majority of our Assemblies of God churches are far too sophisticated for sawdust and crude benches. We don't have people yelling, running around, or jumping over pews. Our pastors have had far more training than most of the leaders of generations ago. Our music is often a professional quality. But do we have the fire of God in our midst? What would the fire look like today ... in this culture, in our context, with the excellent Bible training and God-given resources available to us?

My daughter Eden experiences a Spirit-filled church in our congregation, but it is far different from the one my great-grandmother attended. On Sunday mornings, Eden walks into the room and people greet her warmly. There are no cliques of insiders who are Spirit-filled and outsiders who aren't. The warmth of God's grace, not judgment, is the atmosphere of the room. When the service starts, she enjoys exuberant (but not out of control or odd) praise and worship. The worship team has prayed and asked God for direction for the music. As they lead, they are very conscious that it's far more than a musical performance; they are leading people in offering a sacrifice of praise to the One who deserves all honor and glory. We value excellence in the performing arts, but only to point to the beauty of Christ and eliminate distractions, not to impress anyone. The worship team is open to the Lord's leading during the time of singing. If the leader senses that God wants him to change directions, he follows God's leading. The time of singing, then, is Spirit-directed during the planning and preparation, and Spirit-empowered and Spirit-led during the service.

The leeway is to make room for the Spirit to speak to us in any way He chooses, but cultural sensitivity requires us to have a reasonable and predictable time to end the service.

As worship continues, we give brief but clear instructions to avoid interrupting anyone who is speaking (including the speaker) and to avoid speaking over people in tongues.[17] We always leave time for God to speak to us through a prophetic word or during a time of silence when God speaks to everyone individually. Due to multiple services, our services last between an hour and fifteen minutes and an hour and a half. (Others may choose an hour to an hour and fifteen minutes.) The leeway is to make room for the Spirit to speak to us in any way He chooses, but cultural sensitivity requires us to have a reasonable and predictable time to end the service. This, of course, doesn't mean we plan on fifteen minutes of dead time during the service. We simply allow this interval to respond as the Lord leads—to go a little longer to continue a song that is particularly meaningful, to invite someone to give a prophetic word, an expression of tongues with interpretations, or to be silent and listen to the Lord's whisper. The fifteen minutes is "planned spiritual flexibility and responsiveness." At the end of this time, there may be a sense of wonder or of peace, but never chaos.

Pastors and other church leaders need to avoid measuring the value of the worship service by the number or quality of the expression of the gifts. We can't say the Lord didn't accomplish His purposes if no one spoke in tongues or prophesied. God is always speaking, but not at our bidding and often not according to our expectations. Sometimes, He speaks most powerfully during a time of quiet prayer, through a song, or in the words of the sermon. There is no rigid formula. God is much too big to be contained in any box we create for Him.

We believe that if we do church without giving God time to speak, we may be telling Him and those who are attending that we don't believe we need Him at all.

After the time of being open to the expression of the gifts, the fire of God's presence is readily apparent. The preaching is designed to "keep in step with the Spirit" to bring people closer to God, inspire faith, convict of sin, glorify God, and point people to Jesus as the only hope of salvation. As the pastor, I always want to end with a challenge for people to respond to God. This challenge may take the form of a question they can consider privately or talk about with their families over lunch, or I may ask them to respond by taking a step of obedience according to the passage we've examined. I may ask people to come forward to accept Christ as their Savior or to respond to the message in another way, but I rarely give people the opportunity to be baptized in the Holy Spirit on Sunday morning. This doesn't mean, however, that people don't get baptized in the Holy Spirit in our regular worship services. People often are baptized in the Spirit on Sunday morning—in our times of worship, at the end of the service as they talk to someone at the front, or through praying with a friend. We just don't have long times of praying at the altar for the baptism in the Spirit because it's not normally the time or place for this to happen in our culture.

My goal—and my prayer—is that God will break through to people on Sunday morning with a powerful sense of His presence. I don't want them to just check off the box that they attended church so they can earn a couple of points with God. That's not a response to God's amazing grace, and it's not the work of the Spirit. If people don't experience the fire of God on Sunday morning, they probably won't experience Him the rest of the week. I hope the fire they sense on Sunday keeps them hot all week! It's my responsibility to be hot all week so we create an environment on Sunday that God can use to touch people with the Spirit's fire, nothing less than that.

My daughter Eden may not realize it, but people have been asking God to anoint the speaker and every aspect of the service. Hopefully, she senses God speaking directly to her in every part of it. Each element of the service is carefully planned under the guidance of God, but we are completely open to the Lord changing the direction we're going.

The events on Sunday morning, though, are only the most visible demonstrations of the fire. On a cold, winter night when Shelli and I are having people over to our house, I don't wait until they arrive to light the fire in the fireplace. Long before they ring the doorbell, I gather the logs, find the kindling, make sure the flue is clear, and open the damper. About thirty minutes or an hour before they arrive, I light the fire so that it's established, glowing, and warm when they walk through the door. Another reason I prepare before they come is that I don't want to be scrambling around and have dirty hands when they show up. I want to be fully prepared to welcome them warmly.

Some might complain that this kind of careful preparation—in building a fire for guests, or more particularly, in crafting a church service—robs the pastor and his people of spontaneity and quenches the Spirit. I understand the reasoning, but I believe that I can be more sensitive and responsive to the Spirit in a service if my mind and heart have been in tune with Him all week. And it's not just me. During the week, everyone on our team and those who are in our "core" of people who are committed to pray ask God to show up in power and love. If the fire is burning all week in our preparation and prayers, it will burn even more brightly and with more heat during the service. We aren't quenching the fire; we're building a fireplace.

We don't need sawdust or benches, off-key singing, shouting, or poorly prepared teaching to prove we're dependent on the Spirit. We only need the genuine fire of God, a little sensitivity to our culture, and a commitment to be good shepherds. Some might claim that our suggestions accommodate the culture too much, while others say we aren't sensitive enough to the culture. We admit that it's not easy to find the right balance. Jesus never watered down His message, but He went from town to town to speak to people where He found them. He both gave the stark summons to lay down our lives to follow Him and was as tender as a mother in His love for misfits, outcasts, children, and foreigners. Most of us have struggled to find the right way to communicate our traditional teaching in a relevant way today. We've struggled, too, so we're offering a framework we have found helpful.

Many pastors are afraid they'll turn people off and run them away if the gifts are expressed on Sunday morning. I (Scott) often get some exercise by running with a man who attends our church. One morning, he looked like he had something on his mind. After a few minutes, he asked, "Pastor, can I talk to you about something?"

My mind raced with the myriad of possible topics he might bring up. I assured him he could talk to me about anything. It wasn't at all what I expected. He said, "I have some neighbors I'd like to bring to church. They don't know the Lord, and I want them to hear a clear message of the gospel. My wife and I have been building a relationship with them, and their son plays with our son." He paused for a second, and then continued, "But since we've been expressing the gifts in church, I . . . I don't know if we can bring them. I'm afraid they'll freak out!"

I completely understood. I was at the same place only a few years before. I asked my friend, "Do we ever express the gifts without teaching people about them first?" He shook his head and looked a little more encouraged. I then reminded him, "We've made a commitment to always do everything decently and in an orderly manner. Haven't you seen that every week?"

"Yeah!" he answered with an expression of hope. "Maybe it won't be so bad after all!"

A week passed, and we planned to go running again. As soon as he saw me, he almost exploded with his news: "Pastor Scott, you won't believe it! Our neighbors went to church last Sunday. We didn't invite them to go with us. They just went on their own. I guess they'd heard us talk about The Oaks and how much it's meant to us. We didn't even know they were there until we looked down during the altar time. They were all there receiving Christ—the husband, the wife, and their son!"

I couldn't help it. I had to smile and say, "Well, I guess they weren't too freaked out, huh?"

He laughed, "No, not at all."

Sometimes, we're more scared than the people we're trying to protect. God puts a longing in their hearts for a genuine spiritual experience. When they see it and sense it, they respond to God's gracious invitation.

Yes, the supernatural is strange. Who would have thought that the Almighty God who lived in matchless glory would step out of heaven to become a human being—and not a powerful ruler but a humble servant, so humble that He submitted to humiliation, unjust persecution, and a shameful execution? Who would have thought that the One who died as the lowest criminal would come back to life three days later? And the greatest marvel of all: Who would have thought that He would entrust His enterprise of redeeming the world to the ones who had run for their lives? The Bible describes a God of miracles and glory and a church that experiences supernatural love, forgiveness, and power. He is the One we serve. He is the One who still amazes people today.

Some preachers ought to put more fire into their sermons, or more sermons into the fire.

—Vance Havner

CONSIDER THIS . . .

1. What are some evidences of "false fire"?

2. What are some distractions and distresses that threaten to quench the fire in pastors? Which ones are problems for you?

3. What would you expect (benefits and fears) if you scheduled time every Sunday morning service for the Spirit to speak?

6 IGNITING THE FIRE

A few years ago a Chinese house church leader commented, "When Chinese believers read the book of Acts, we see in it our own experience; when foreign Christians read the book of Acts, they see in it inspiring stories."

—Robert Menzies

IF THE BAPTISM IN THE HOLY SPIRIT NO LONGER FITS ON SUNDAY nights because of our culture, and if it doesn't work on Sunday mornings, when and how can pastors make this teaching and experience a vital part of the church? At our churches, Freedom Fellowship International (FFI) and The Oaks Fellowship, we've created different events so this priority takes its rightful place in church life.

FORMS AND FUNCTIONS

At The Oaks, Wednesday night prayer services have replaced what used to happen on Sunday nights. Every Wednesday night, I (Scott) or another pastor lead people in praying in the Spirit and invite those who have never been baptized in the Spirit to come forward for prayer. Elders and other leaders gather around them to lay hands on them and pray. Almost every week, at least a few people are baptized in the Spirit in this prayer meeting.

Once a month in this meeting, brief and specific teaching on the baptism in the Holy Spirit is the focal point of the message. One Wednesday night every two months, the entire message is devoted to teaching the nature and work of the Holy Spirit, the history of the baptism in the Spirit in Acts, what to expect when someone has the experience, what it means to speak in a prayer language, and how the experience deepens and heightens every aspect of intimacy, obedience, and service. Of course, on each of these occasions, the message is followed by an invitation to come forward for prayer to receive the baptism in the Spirit.

At FFI, a weekend experiential workshop called Freedom Quest is held three to four times a year from a Friday night to Saturday about 5:00 p.m. The event is held at a hotel so people can get away from distractions and concentrate on absorbing and applying the principles. Each person who attends is paired with a trained mentor. The sessions are pointed and profound, exposing past wounds and sins, expressing the assurance of God's grace and forgiveness, the deception of the Enemy, our new identity in Christ, overcoming strongholds and fears, and presenting the steps of spiritual growth. At the end of this event, people are as spiritually cleansed and open as they've ever been in their lives. At that point, they are open to a deeper work of the Spirit, so the pastors teach them about the baptism in the Spirit in the last session before they leave. They are invited to join FFI's weekly Saturday evening Core, which includes people who are committed to pray. Those who are coming from the Freedom Quest are asked if they'd like to receive the baptism in the Holy Spirit. At this point, the mentor and a person or two from Core lay hands on them and pray. Almost invariably, these people receive the baptism in the Spirit at that moment. For the next twelve weeks, the person meets with a mentor for additional teaching, training, and steps of growth.[18]

At other churches, pastors may choose to conduct a series of four or five classes two or three times a year to teach people about the baptism in the Spirit and invite people to have the experience. Some pastors may choose to encourage small group leaders to teach this truth and invite people into the experience, but this requires the pastor to make wise selections of group leaders and then equip them adequately.

No matter what form this teaching and the experience take in a particular church, this emphasis needs to have these components:

- Clear teaching for interested people so they understand the Scriptures and have clear expectations when they experience the baptism in the Spirit,

- Informed, trained, and compassionate mentors to pray with people and answer questions before and after an experience, and

- Regular reinforcement that the baptism in the Spirit is just the beginning of a life of deeper love for God, closer communication with Him, and a greater desire to serve.

Note: This video-based curriculum is available at core.theoaksonline.org.

It's wise for pastors to regularly weave teaching about the baptism in the Spirit into their messages, just as they regularly speak on other topics like forgiveness, generosity, integrity, prayer, obedience, and reaching out to the lost and the least. Do the principles of the Spirit-filled life apply to these topics? Of course they do. Keeping in step with the Spirit in all of these crucial areas shines a light on deception so we can repent, purifies our motives, directs our choices, and empowers our actions. The Spirit-filled life applies to every aspect of life.

In Acts, people received the baptism in the Spirit in three distinct ways. Some experienced the baptism when they were praying (Acts 2:1-4 and 4:31); some experienced it in response to the preaching of the Word (Acts 10:44-46); and others experienced it when someone laid hands on them (Acts 8:14-17, 9:17, and 19:1-6). The Lord can work in extremely creative ways. One Sunday, I (Scott) spoke on what parents can do to model and impart the principles of a Spirit-filled life to their children, including praying in the Spirit for their kids and letting them listen. That day, a couple couldn't attend church because both of them were sick, so they watched it streaming online. Their niece was visiting from out of town, and she watched with them. After the service, she looked at them and said, "I don't have what Pastor Scott was talking about." The couple explained more about the baptism in the Spirit, and then they laid hands on her in the living room and prayed. She was baptized in the Spirit right there!

THE INVITATION

In the Freedom Quest at FFI and on Wednesday nights at The Oaks, we emphasize the *benefits* of being baptized in the Holy Spirit, not the *necessity*. In past generations, pastors often communicated that people "must" be baptized in the Spirit and speak in tongues to prove themselves as legitimate Pentecostals. This sometimes seemed manipulative, and it tended to produce a two-tiered spirituality of insiders and outsiders. As we've pointed out, sometimes pastors have promoted the experience with particular people because they needed board slots filled and being baptized in the Spirit was a requirement for those positions. That's not the motive we find in the Scriptures.

Today, however, many people who come to our churches aren't from a Pentecostal background, so we can't make too many assumptions about what they already know about the baptism in the Spirit.

We teach the essentials of the nature and work of the Spirit of God, and we examine the pattern found in Acts of Spirit baptism and the experience of tongues. We explain that the baptism is an open door to a richer, deeper, stronger relationship with God. We anticipate the common questions people ask, and we invite them to ask any additional questions about issues we haven't addressed to their satisfaction. Some people have been attending an Assemblies of God church for years, but for any number of reasons, they haven't understood and experienced the baptism in the Spirit. Today, however, many people who come to our churches aren't from a Pentecostal background, so we can't make too many assumptions about what they already know about the baptism in the Spirit. Many are Catholics or Baptists or from another mainline denomination. A few have been taught that the sign gifts have ceased; however, most are interested but uninformed. All of them need solid Bible teaching and patient explanations.

Being baptized in the Spirit is one of the most holy and intimate moments in a person's life. We stay away from theatrics. Yelling and commanding may have been common years ago, but we've found a better way. We treat it as a tender pastoral moment to gently lead people into the presence and power of a gracious King. My (John's) personal experience was a beautiful moment. When I was a boy, I was at a prayer meeting, and I was hungry for God. I sensed the tug of the Spirit to go forward and be baptized in the Spirit. A young woman smiled at me and asked, "Would you like to do this, John?"

I nodded and responded, "Yes, I think so."

She said, "Good. Raise your hands. I'm going to pray for you, and new words will come out of your mouth." It happened just as she said. It was a wonderful, sensitive, beautiful moment. I cherish the experience, and it shapes how I teach people and invite them to be baptized in the Spirit.

At our church, we explain that each person has a choice. God doesn't twist our arms, and we don't have to twist His arm. He delights to give us good gifts! Jesus told His disciples, "If you then, though you are evil, know how to give good gifts to your children, how much more will your Father in heaven give the Holy Spirit to those who ask him!" (Luke 11:13) God invites us to take His hand and trust Him.

Being baptized in the Spirit is a parallel to water baptism. When people are baptized in water, they don't stand on the side. They have to take a step into the pool or lake or river and get wet. In the same way, we can't stand on the side and expect something to magically happen. We have to take a step—this time, not to get wet, but to get hot with the fire of God!

For each person, this treasured moment doesn't happen in a vacuum. The role of the pastor and other leaders is creating an environment of love, warmth, and expectancy. Before the event, people have been praying that God will show up in love and strength so that He is evident to each person in the room. As the worship leader is singing and the pastor is speaking, the warmth of God emanates from them. The pastor and all who have been praying anticipate God's mighty work, and the people who attend often sense the love, joy, peace, and power flowing through each person who has a part in the meeting.

We explain that we will focus on the grace of God made known through the sacrifice of Jesus for us. As we praise Him, He will baptize in the Spirit those who want more of Him.

At the invitation, those who are interested come forward. Usually, only one person joins each one of them to lay hands on that person and pray. (We don't want there to be any additional pressure to perform for a large group.) We suggest they raise their hands and praise Jesus out loud.

If they want, they can close their eyes to block out any distractions as they pray. We explain, "As you pray, you're going to sense God's presence and warmth because you're drawing closer to the fire. Your experience with God's fire may not be exactly like another person's, but you'll sense His warmth."

In this pivotal moment, many people have a sense of resistance. We explain that this is completely normal, but it's only a "speed bump." When we drive in a parking lot, we often encounter a speed bump. We see it coming, so when we encounter it, we push past it and keep going. In the same way, people who are approaching the new, thrilling experience of being baptized in the Holy Spirit often have a sense of resistance at the moment they sense God's presence and anticipate speaking in their own, new prayer language. It's not a massive wall; it's just a speed bump to go over. When we explain this common phenomenon to them, they often sigh with relief and feel more comfortable moving forward.

We have trained our Core and other leaders to pastor this precious moment in the lives of those who have come forward. When they join a person at the front, they may repeat our instructions and suggestions to raise their hands and praise Jesus out loud. If a mentor senses resistance, they can again relate the concept of the speed bump to reassure the person. The mentor often then explains, "I'm going to pray in the Spirit while you praise Jesus. God will give you another language as we pray. Your language will be a bit different than what you hear from me. It will be your own."

Quite often, the person begins praying in a spirit language very soon after the mentor begins praying. It may surprise the person how free, easy, and delightful it is. Sometimes, though, there is a delay. The mentor may share the passage when Jesus healed the blind man, but it took two stages. First, the man reported, "I see people; they look like trees walking around." To Jesus, the delay wasn't a big deal. He wasn't shocked. He didn't blame the man, and He didn't blame himself. He again laid hands on the man's eyes, and this time, "his eyes were opened, his sight was restored, and he saw everything clearly" (Mark 8:24-25).

We've trained our leaders and mentors to pastor the moment of delay. There is no panic, no anxiety, and no condemnation—just patience and love. They can say, "Tell me what's going on with you right now? What are you feeling? What do you sense?"

The person may express uncertainty:

- "I'm scared of losing control."

- "What if this doesn't work?"

- "I don't think I'm clean enough. I have some things that aren't right with God."

- "I'm afraid I won't be able to control this when it starts happening."

- "I heard somebody speak in tongues one time. It was really loud and bizarre. Is that what I'm going to do?"

- "I've heard people fall down. Am I going to fall down?"

- "I'm feeling something I've never felt before, and it scares me."

- "All this is weird to me. I don't even know if I want this to happen."

When a person doesn't immediately experience the baptism, some pastors and other leaders feel pressured to make the experience happen right away. They may give advice, such as "Just pray some more," or "Pray louder," or say this or that over and over again. Instead, we recommend that the leader or mentor pastor the person by having a loving conversation about what's going on. Quite often, a quiet conversation reveals a fear that needs to surface and be soothed or perhaps pride that has become a barrier to the person being open to the Spirit. There is no blaming and no shaming. We simply say, "Help me understand what you're thinking and feeling. I'd like to help you." Then we listen . . . and listen some more. When they feel heard and understood, they relax and trust the mentor and the Lord so they can take the next step.

Loving the person is far more important than getting a notch of success in getting another person baptized in the Spirit.

There's no pressure to make anything happen at that moment. Loving the person is far more important than getting a notch of success in getting another person baptized in the Spirit. The leader and the inquirer can sit and talk for a while, and if concerns aren't answered, they can meet sometime during the week or the following Sunday to continue the conversation. There's no rush in the least. It's all about loving people enough to patiently answer their questions. In fact, the way we treat them at their moment of speed bumps or prolonged hesitation may say more to them about us and the church than anything else they experience in our services. Pastor the moment. Love is patient and kind.

ONE EXAMPLE

I (John) talked to a young woman named Maggie who was interested in being baptized in the Spirit, but she had many questions. She came from a church background that had no experience of Spirit baptism, but she longed for a closer relationship with God. We were at a conference where Scott and I had just spoken about the baptism in the Holy Spirit. During a break, she began asking me a series of questions. I answered each one and invited her to ask any more she wanted to ask.

She came to me with a strong hope coupled with concerns. She asked, "How do I go from praying in English to praying in a different prayer language?"

I explained that God would give her the new language as she praised Jesus. It wasn't something she had to generate.

"When can this happen?" she asked.

I assured her, "Anytime you want it to happen."

"You mean, like now?"

I almost laughed, "Yes, like now." We found a quiet corner of the room, and I explained what was going to happen. She admitted, "But something in me feels . . ."

"Hesitant?" I completed her sentence.

She looked pleasantly surprised and responded, "Yes, that's it. I feel hesitant!" She felt understood and validated.

I explained the concept of the speed bump, and she was relieved. "It's entirely normal," I assured her. "Don't let it stop you. Push over it."

I offered to pray for her and with her, and she agreed. I told her to praise Jesus softly. I told her I was going to pray in the Spirit, and in a moment, she would realize she was speaking in a new language. Hers would be a new language, probably with only a few syllables like a baby's first words, but I assured her that her prayer language would develop as she used it. We never prompt people to "say Jesus real fast" or copy our language or anything similar. That's manipulation, not the baptism in the Spirit. God doesn't need our help to give people a new language.

Maggie began mixing new syllables with her English prayers of praise. When I heard her, I affirmed, "This is it. You're there." Seconds later, she began praying entirely in a new language. After a minute or so, I touched her arm. She looked up with an expression of pure joy. I smiled back and asked, "What just happened?" I wanted her to articulate her experience for me so she could tell others later. Also, many people have doubts about their experience only minutes after it, and I wanted to confirm what had just happened to her.

She said, "As I prayed, I imagined going over a speed bump, and then it just happened. I was praying to God in a new language!"

I asked, "Do you think this is something you can do on your own?"

Maggie answered, "I don't know."

I responded, "Try it now. You can pray, but I'm not going to pray with you."

Maggie bowed her head and began praising Jesus. Almost immediately, she began praying in tongues. A moment later, I stopped her. She beamed! I told her, "You've been baptized in the Spirit, and you have your own prayer language." She nodded, and I continued, "You've been speaking very softly. Do you think you could add just a bit more volume to your prayer to speak in a normal tone like we're talking right now, or would that make you uncomfortable?"

She shook her head and said, "No, that would be fine."

Maggie prayed again in her new language, but this time, it was at a normal conversational volume. I stopped her after a minute. She was thrilled. Then she asked, "What do I do now?"

I answered, "Just keep using your language to pray to God every day, and enjoy the warmth of His love."

I didn't try to explain that she could ask God for an interpretation to her prayers. That would come later. This moment was a beautiful, sacred time for Maggie, and I wanted her to savor it.

Later, she told me that when she drove home in her car, she gave full voice to her new language, and the love of God overwhelmed her. Tears of joy flowed down her face as she drove her car through traffic.

CONFIRMATION BY MENTORS

Part of our teaching to those who want to be baptized in the Spirit is to prepare them for what happens after the experience. Quite often, this powerful and tender moment is often followed by a toxic flood of self-doubt: *Was it real? Am I a fool? What will people think of me? What if I can't make it happen again? Was it all just manipulation?* This is a vulnerable time in the life of each person who experiences the baptism in the Spirit. The Enemy and the flesh will try to get them to discount the experience and conclude it was phony and ridiculous. We need to do whatever we can to help them solidify what the Lord has done in their lives.

Just as it's the pastor's responsibility and privilege to teach clearly and create a loving, warm environment for people to respond in faith to be baptized in the Spirit, it's important for him to shepherd people through the coming weeks and months to establish them in their new level of intimacy with God. Depending on the size of the church, a pastor may not be present in the life of every person who responds. Mentors, group leaders, and others need to be trained to care for people during this crucial period of their lives. In our tradition, the pastor has been the chief (or only) voice to instruct and invite people to experience the baptism in the Spirit, but we will be far more effective—and relationships will be stronger throughout the body—if we equip others and let them shepherd people in and after this beautiful moment. If the pastor tries to do it all, he won't be sensitive to each person's hopes and fears, so some will feel misunderstood and pressured. Enlisting godly mentors helps to solve this problem ... and it broadens the leadership base of the church, which multiplies enthusiasm, service, and care.

We will be wise if we avoid making assumptions about who is a capable mentor or shepherd. Many of those who have leadership responsibilities in our churches don't have the specific understanding of the questions and issues that arise immediately after the baptism in the Spirit. It's our job to identify competent, compassionate, available people who can step into the lives of others and help them grow. At FFI, the ones who help people after they are baptized in the Spirit are the same ones who mentored them before the event at the Freedom Quest. It's a seamless relationship.

The Oaks and other churches have a different system of training leaders and connecting them with people. There are many different scenarios that can work, but the principle is important: Equip people to be mentors and connect them with those who are baptized in the Spirit. For many pastors, this is the most important shift in strategy and planning. Instead of being the lone gun, we identify, train and delegate a growing number of men and women whom God will use to touch many lives.

People need to understand that the experience they just had is the beginning, not the end. It's not even the high point; there are many more wonderful experiences to come. As they walk in the fullness of the Spirit, they'll have a deeper, wider, richer relationship with God. They'll learn to flow in the gifts: They'll begin to prophesy, God will give them interpretation when they speak in tongues, they'll tap into the wisdom and discernment given only by the Spirit, and they'll see God do miraculous things.

One of the things we teach the people at our churches is that the fire of the Holy Spirit may look very different in people's lives. God has given us different backgrounds, different personalities, different roles, and different circumstances. Fireplaces in houses range from rustic stone to ornately carved marble, but all of them are places where fire can burn. In the same way, we don't compare our experiences and expressions of God's fire, and we don't compete with each other. We celebrate the differences as evidence of God's wonderful creativity.

In the Preface to his translation of Acts, *The Young Church in Action,* J. B. Phillips wrote these words:

> It is impossible to spend several months in close study of the remarkable short book . . . without being profoundly stirred and, to be honest, disturbed. The reader is stirred because he is seeing Christianity, the real thing, in action for the first time in human history. The newborn Church, as vulnerable as any human child, having neither money, influence, nor power in the ordinary sense, is setting forth joyfully and courageously to win the pagan world for God through Christ. . . . Yet we cannot help feeling disturbed as well as moved, for this surely is the Church as it was meant to be. It is vigorous and flexible, for these are the days before it ever became fat and short of breath through prosperity, or muscle-bound by over-organization. These men did not make "acts of faith," they believed; they did not "say their prayers," they really prayed. They did not hold conferences on

psychosomatic medicine, they simply healed the sick. But if they were uncomplicated and naive by modern standards, we have ruefully to admit that they were open on the God-ward side in a way that is almost unknown today.

CONSIDER THIS . . .

1. As you think about the options for creating an environment to teach people about the baptism in the Spirit and invite them to respond, what do you think would work best for your church? Explain why.

2. What are some factors that cause people to feel manipulated and pressured when they come to be baptized in the Holy Spirit? Does the gentle, personal approach described in this chapter appeal to you? Why or why not?

3. What are the benefits and costs of identifying, training, and delegating responsibilities to mentors who can shepherd people possibly before but certainly during their experience of receiving and after they receive the baptism in the Spirit?

7 EVERY ROOM IN THE PALACE

The Spirit-filled life is not a special, deluxe edition of Christianity. It is part and parcel of the total plan of God for His people.

—A. W. Tozer

WHEN PEOPLE TRUST IN JESUS CHRIST AS SAVIOR, THEY ARE rescued "from the domain of darkness and brought into the kingdom of the Son ... in whom we have redemption, the forgiveness of sins" (Col. 1:13-14). They are issued a new passport because their citizenship has changed (Phil. 3:20). They aren't brought into a shack or a hut; they are brought into God's palace!

Every person who is born again—no matter the age, from Pentecost to today, no matter the denomination or tradition, and no matter the continent, ethnicity, or financial status—experiences the blessings and benefits of salvation. They are chosen and adopted by the Father, forgiven by Christ, and sealed by the Holy Spirit (Eph. 1:4-14). Their status and destiny have been radically changed (Eph. 2:1-8; 2 Cor. 5:1-10), and their motivations have been turned inside out. They no longer live for success, pleasure, and approval but for the One who paid the ultimate price for them. The love of God floods their hearts and energizes everything they do.

Paul connects our new motives to Christ's sacrifice: "For Christ's love compels us, because we are convinced that one died for all, and therefore all died. And he died for all, that those who live should no longer live for themselves but for him who died for them and was raised again" (2 Cor. 5:14-15). The things that break God's heart begin to break theirs, and the things that thrill God thrill them. They increasingly devote their time, energy, and money to reach the lost and care for the least (2 Cor. 5:11-21 and Matt. 25:35-36).

If we use the metaphor of a palace, every person who believes in Christ is invited into the foyer, the family room, the kitchen, and the bedrooms. They can live comfortably and enjoy the incredible blessings of being a son or daughter of the King. The baptism in the Spirit doesn't make anyone a superior Christian, any more loved, or any more of a citizen of God's kingdom, but it opens doors into rooms where the nine sign gifts can be experienced and used for the glory of God. Every child of God is invited to open those doors, but they have to receive the key.

Let's repeat the point: The experience of the fullness of the Spirit and the expression of the nine gifts doesn't make anyone more of a Christian or a better Christian. In fact, those who believe they are superior because they have experienced the baptism in the Spirit display arrogance that is the opposite of the fruit of the Spirit! The gifts aren't designed to feed our thirst for power, prestige, or superior experience. They remind us of God's greatness and glory. Paradoxically, they quench our thirst for God and make us even thirstier for Him. When we encounter the Spirit of grace and truth, we love Christ more than ever, are more humble because we realize the source is God, support the body of Christ by our gifts, and have more of the heart of Jesus to reach out beyond our comfort zone to love and serve others in the community and around the world.

We know plenty of people who haven't been baptized in the Spirit but love God and serve Him more faithfully and passionately than many who have had the baptism experience. There are no second-class Christians. We can all learn from one another even if we come from different traditions, but only if we're humble enough to ask and seek.

The baptism in the Spirit gives us a closer communication with God than we have ever had before, but we never discount the spiritual experience of any believer. Love for God, a heart for the lost, and obedience out of gratitude aren't reserved for Pentecostals.

Tradition gives us some security, but it can't replace a humble heart. That was the problem with the religious leaders of Jesus' day. We've already looked at John the Baptist's promise that the Messiah was coming, and He would baptize people in the Holy Spirit and fire, but the context of John's remarks is revealing. Matthew sets the scene:

> But when he saw many of the Pharisees and Sadducees coming to where he was baptizing, he said to them: "You brood of vipers! Who warned you to flee from the coming wrath? Produce fruit in keeping with repentance. And do not think you

SPREAD THE FIRE

can say to yourselves, 'We have Abraham as our father.' I tell you that out of these stones God can raise up children for Abraham. The ax is already at the root of the trees, and every tree that does not produce good fruit will be cut down and thrown into the fire." (Matt. 3:7-10)

In our fellowship, we can find both ends of the spectrum: Some are wedded to the form of our historical traditions and are resistant to cultural relevance, but others are committed to relevance and have left behind the beauty, power, and heart of those traditions.

THE FRUIT, NOT THE FLASH

The baptism in the Spirit isn't primarily about the experience of the gifts; it's about having a deeper, richer love for God, displayed in glad and sacrificial service. We are wise, then, to point people in our teaching back to the work of the Spirit in the lives of all believers—the role the Spirit plays in all the rooms of the palace.

CONVICTING AND CLEANSING

Before Jesus was arrested, tried, and executed, He taught His disciples many truths. They had a hard time grasping the fact that He and the Father are both God. Exasperated and confused, Philip told Him, "Lord, show us the Father and that will be enough for us" (John 14:8). Jesus patiently explained His nature (again), "Anyone who has seen me has seen the Father. . . . I am in the Father, and . . . the Father is in me" (John 14:8-10). They had difficulty swallowing two divine persons, but Jesus blew their minds by explaining there are three! "And I will ask the Father, and he will give you another advocate to help you and be with you forever—the Spirit of truth" (John 14:16-17).

In his first letter, John explains that Jesus is our advocate before the Father in heaven. When we sin, Jesus is our defense attorney. He doesn't plead for mercy. Instead, He points to the fact that the penalty has already been completely paid (1 John 2:1-2). On that night with the disciples, Jesus was saying, "I'm leaving. I know you don't want Me to go, but I'm going so the Spirit can come to fulfill His role. I'll be your advocate at the right hand of the Father, and the Holy Spirit will be your advocate here on earth. He will represent the Father and Me in everything He does. Trust Him." (See John 16:5-6, 12-15.) Jesus explained in these words:

> "Unless I go away, the Advocate will not come to you; but if I go, I will send him to you. When he comes, he will prove the world to be in the wrong about sin and righteousness and judgment: about sin, because people do not believe in me; about righteousness, because I am going to the Father, where you can see me no longer; and about judgment, because the prince of this world now stands condemned." (John 16:7-11)

Sin, righteousness, and judgment: From the day of Pentecost, the Holy Spirit has made Christ known to us in these three crucial ways:

- He has taught us about the presence and destructive-ness of sin in thoughts, words, and deeds. When we realize the reality of sin, we "come to our senses" like the younger brother in Jesus' parable (Luke 15), and we can repent.

- He teaches us about the pure and perfect righteous-ness of Christ, which was finally and fully demonstrated by His resurrection, ascension, and His seat at the right hand of the Father. Some of the people who saw Jesus when He walked the earth may have thought He was an ordinary man, maybe a revolutionary, but nothing more than that. But those who might see Him now—like Stephen saw Him as he died (Acts 7:54-56)—would be under no such delusions!

- He teaches us about God's righteous judgment. There will come a day when the sheep are separated from the goats, and those who have chosen to live for them-selves will be cast into outer darkness (Matt. 25:30-46). The fire of the Spirit gives us compassion for those who are headed toward the fire of eternal punishment.

ALL TRUTH

On the night He was betrayed, Jesus made a promise to the bewildered men:

"I have much more to say to you, more than you can now bear. But when he, the Spirit of truth, comes, he will guide you into all the truth. He will not speak on his own; he will speak only what he hears, and he will tell you what is yet to come. He will glorify me because it is from me that he will receive what he will make known to you. All that belongs to the Father is mine. That is why I said the Spirit will receive from me what he will make known to you." (John 16:12-15)

The Spirit delights to reveal the truth about God, ourselves, other people, His purposes, and circumstances.

Just as Jesus was "full of grace and truth" (John 1:14), the Holy Spirit is "the Spirit of truth." On that night, the disciples couldn't handle all the truth Jesus wanted to impart to them, but the Spirit would impart it later. In this passage, Jesus was talking about several dimensions of truth in the Holy Spirit's ministry of revelation. The Eleven would (finally) understand the purpose of Christ's life and the meaning of His death, the Spirit would guide all the writers of the New Testament, and He would impart prophetic words, knowledge, and wisdom to those who seek them. The first two are finished and completed, but the third is recorded in the book of Acts and still continues today. The Spirit delights to reveal the truth about God, ourselves, other people, His purposes, and circumstances. The Spirit will take us into every room in the palace and show us how to live as children of the King! In every room, the Spirit will show us more of the matchless wonder of Christ's glory. We'll be amazed, and we'll love every minute of it.

One of the amazing insights in this passage is that the Father has given His treasures to Jesus, and the Spirit makes sure we receive treasures, too. The most valuable treasure is the love of God. A little later on that night, Jesus prayed to prepare His heart and put us in God's hands. He prayed, "The same glory you gave me, I gave them. . . . And give the godless world evidence that you've sent me and loved them in the same way you've loved me" (John 17:22-23, *The Message*). So, one of the goals of the Spirit is to thoroughly convince us that the Father loves us as much as He loves the Son!

The treasures we receive are the unimaginable riches of the Spirit's love, power, and wisdom. In his first letter to the Corinthians, Paul quoted a climactic passage from Isaiah's glowing prophecy of restoration: "No one's ever seen or heard anything like this, never so much as imagined anything quite like it—what God has arranged for those who love him." And Paul makes the point for the Corinthians and for us, "But *you've* seen and heard it because God by his Spirit has brought it all out into the open before you" (1 Cor. 2:9-10, *The Message*). We don't try to manufacture the gifts of the Spirit. They are supernatural and unexplainable. We don't try to compare our experience to the experience of any other person or group because God works uniquely in and through each person who trusts Him.

The palace is full of wonders, and the Spirit opens all the doors. In his letter to the Christians in Corinth, Paul told them more about what the Spirit reveals:

The Spirit, not content to flit around on the surface, dives into the depths of God, and brings out what God planned all along. Who ever knows what you're thinking and planning except you yourself? The same with God—except that he not only knows what he's thinking, but he lets *us* in on it. God offers a full report on the gifts of life and salvation that he is giving us. We don't have to rely on the world's guesses and opinions. We didn't learn this by reading books or going to school; we learned it from God, who taught us person-to-person through Jesus, and we're passing it on to you in the same firsthand, personal way. (1 Cor. 2:10–13 *The Message*)

The Spirit puts us in touch with the deep things of God, and He changes us from the inside out. We no longer see obedience as a grind; we are thrilled to be part of the family business and represent God in all we do. It's a privilege, not a crushing burden.

As we read the New Testament, one of the clearest and most pervasive teachings is that the Holy Spirit uses truth to convict people of sin, remind us of Christ's forgiveness, assure us of our new identity as children of God, and give us the power to take steps of faith. Too many times, pastors have taught (or church members have heard what they wanted to hear) that the baptism in the Holy Spirit keeps us from sinning and protects us from suffering. Those are false promises and a misunderstanding of the Spirit's role. The baptism in the Spirit and speaking in tongues aren't collectively a magical touch that suddenly keeps us from sinning. If anything, a new intimacy with God reveals the hidden sins we've excused or denied for years, and He continues to peel back the layers of deception (like layers of an onion) for the rest of our lives as we walk with Him. Far from becoming immune to sin, we become more sensitive to sin and more grateful for God's forgiveness. Similarly, as we grow in our faith, we are no longer shocked when we encounter setbacks and heartaches. We don't blame God, and we don't necessarily blame ourselves. We are open to any conviction from the Spirit that we have been all or part of the cause. To the extent that it's the result of our selfishness, we repent—but not out of fear. We are like children responding to the patient correction of a loving parent.

The baptism in the Spirit and speaking in tongues aren't collectively a magical touch that suddenly keeps us from sinning. If anything, a new intimacy with God reveals the hidden sins we've excused or denied for years.

Sometimes, though, we suffer from the sins of others or from accidents or natural disasters. We may not know the reason these things have happened, and the Spirit may never reveal the cause (Job never knew in this life), but we can be certain that the cause isn't that God is punishing us.

We can be certain of that because Christ took all our punishment on the cross. God, then, must have some other reason, a higher purpose for our suffering, and in that confidence, we trust Him.

REAL FRUIT

Many Christians have it wrong . . . dead wrong. They think trying hard and being disciplined produce a life that honors God. They define "holiness" as sinlessness, so they walk around continually ashamed (because they're so aware of their failures), proud (when they think they're doing better than someone else), or afraid (because they fear someone will realize they aren't measuring up). First, holiness isn't sinlessness; it's the desire to know, love, and please God more than anything else. And second, holiness isn't just the product of grim determination. Certainly, discipline plays a role, but a secondary one. Spiritual fruit can only be produced by being connected to the source of vitality—Christ. Look at the way Paul contrasts legalism with supernatural life in the Spirit:

But what happens when we live God's way? He brings gifts into our lives, much the same way that fruit appears in an orchard—things like affection for others, exuberance about life, serenity. We develop a willingness to stick with things, a sense of compassion in the heart, and a conviction that a basic holiness permeates things and people. We find ourselves involved in loyal commitments, not needing to force our way in life, able to marshal and

direct our energies wisely. Legalism is helpless in
bringing this about; it only gets in the way. Among
those who belong to Christ, everything connected
with getting our own way and mindlessly responding to what everyone else calls necessities is killed
off for good—crucified. Since this is the kind of life
we have chosen, the life of the Spirit, let us make
sure that we do not just hold it as an idea in our
heads or a sentiment in our hearts, but work out
its implications in every detail of our lives. (Gal.
5:22-25, *The Message*)

Holiness, then, isn't about our grit and determination
to say no to sin and control our passions; it's about our
availability to live in the fullness of the Spirit and let the
love and power of Christ transform us from the inside out.
Experiencing Him in intimacy, joy, gratitude, and hope
gradually changes us so that we become more like Him. It's
not magic, and it's not self-effort. We learn to love even the
most difficult people as we experience God's love for us
(1 John 4:10-11); we forgive those who have offended us
as we experience God's forgiveness for our offenses (Eph.
4:31-32); and we accept outsiders and misfits because
God has warmly accepted us (Rom. 15:7). The baptism in
the Spirit isn't some kind of holy electrical zap. Instead,
the Spirit gives us a deeper, heart-melting sense of the love,
forgiveness, and acceptance of Jesus Christ. It's that simple
and that profound.

EVERY DETAIL

Paul encouraged the Galatians to work out the implications of the Spirit's work in "every detail" of their lives.

All of his letters give clear directions about how to do that, but perhaps none is as clear as a long passage in his letter to the Ephesians. He uses the metaphor of changing clothes to illustrate the choices we can make every moment of every day. Our "old self" is still with us even after we've trusted in Christ. It is characterized by ignorance, foolishness, hard hearts, insensitivity to the things of God, sensuality, and greed. Paul knows these things don't vanish when we trust in Christ. We are a "double exposure" with both old and new natures present in us. Our choice is to notice the evidence of the old self and treat it like a dirty shirt. We notice it, take it off, and then put on a clean one. Paul wrote, "You were taught, with regard to your former way of life, to put off your old self, which is being corrupted by its deceitful desires; to be made new in the attitude of your minds; and to put on the new self, created to be like God in true righteousness and holiness" (Eph. 4:22–24).

In other words, don't live by the implications of your old identity; live by your new one that is like God! But Paul, the good pastor, knows that many people need more than general principles. He then gives a series of specific insights about how to "put off" and "put on":

- Put off falsehood and put on honesty.

- Put off self-absorbed, unrighteous anger and put on righteous expressions of anger at injustice.

- Put off stealing and put on working and giving to others.

- Put off destructive language and put on words that build people up.

- Put off all expressions of bitterness, rage, and hatred and put on kindness, compassion and forgiveness (Eph. 4:25-32).

In every moment, we face choices. Our human nature pushes us toward selfishness, greed, and revenge, but the Spirit of God reminds us that we have a new identity, a new job description in the kingdom, and a new destiny. As we remember who we are—and especially *whose* we are—we'll have the insight and courage to put on Christ.

The Spirit of God loves us and longs for us to follow Jesus. He weeps when we weep, and He rejoices when we rejoice.

These aren't academic or dry, moralistic choices. They're personal. Near the end of Paul's list of examples of changing clothes, he wrote, "And do not grieve the Holy Spirit of God, with whom you were sealed for the day of redemption" (Eph. 4:30). The Holy Spirit isn't an "it" or an impersonal force. He is a person . . . a person who experiences the full range of emotions from delight to grief. When we sin, He doesn't pounce on us in delight to clobber us. Quite the opposite; His heart is broken, and He grieves over the harm we've experienced and inflicted on others.

We might ignore a speed limit sign because it's impersonal . . . until the patrolman steps out of his car! But the Spirit of God loves us and longs for us to follow Jesus. He weeps when we weep, and He rejoices when we rejoice. When the Spirit convicts us of sin, it's not to blast us with fiery condemnation. With gentleness, He's whispering, "Come back. Come to Me. Experience the cleansing flood of forgiveness, and let My love touch your heart."

Some people may object: "Well, 'don't grieve the Holy Spirit' is the only mention of the Spirit in this part of Paul's letter. Are we supposed to just muscle up and make all this happen on our own?" Today, many people read the Bible episodically and devotionally, and they miss the context of the passage they're reading. Reading the Bible this way is better than not reading at all, but it can be misleading. For example, when Paul describes our spiritual fight "against the rulers, against the authorities, against the powers of this dark world and against spiritual forces of evil in the heavenly realms" in the last chapter of Ephesians, we need to remember that he had already written in the first chapter that Christ's resurrection power is "far above" all those forces, and in chapter three, he explained that the gospel of grace amazes "the rulers and authorities in the heavenly realms." Similarly, the presence and power of the Spirit are woven throughout Paul's letter. Everything God has done, is doing, and wants to do, we can conclude, is a product of the Holy Spirit's work. He has sealed us (Eph. 1:13-14), which signifies ownership and security, so we know we belong to God. Along with Paul, we ask God to give us "the Spirit of wisdom and revelation" so that we may know God better (Eph. 1:17). Reconciled human relationships

154 SPREAD THE FIRE

are a result of our experience of being reconciled to God; love for Him and for them happens only when we experience "power through his Spirit in [our] inner being" (Eph. 3:16). The beautiful blend of unity and diversity in the body of Christ is the Spirit's work (Eph. 4:1–6). So, all that Paul describes in terms of "changing clothes" and making better choices is the result of the Spirit's work in us and through us. To continue making changes that honor God, we need to "keep being filled with the Spirit" (Eph. 5:18) and fight our battles with the Enemy with all the resources the Spirit has given us (Eph. 6:10–20). Paul's admonitions to make repentance a daily (and moment by moment) practice aren't given in a vacuum. He continually points us to the work of the Holy Spirit for security, direction, motivation, and power. When we read (or teach) a passage, we find richer meaning if we notice the broader context, such as Paul's teaching about the Spirit throughout his letter to the Ephesians.

In his letter, Paul's instructions about holy living continue. He tells us to be *sexually pure* (5:3), he says we should have *pure words* coming out of our mouths (5:4), and we are to have *pure relationships* (5:5–7). Again, he points us back to the cross as our foundation and motivation: "For you were once darkness, but now you are light in the Lord. Live as children of light (for the fruit of the light consists in all goodness, righteousness and truth) and find out what pleases the Lord. Have nothing to do with the fruitless deeds of darkness, but rather expose them" (Eph. 5:8–11). We might paraphrase Paul this way: "You aren't who you used to be. You have a new identity, a new source of love and power. Don't go back. There was only emptiness and hopelessness and darkness there. Live your new, Christ-bought, Spirit-empowered life. Settle for nothing less!"

We have become fireplaces to house the fire of the Spirit. It's our incredible privilege to be consumed by the love and power of the Holy Spirit so that gradually, day by day and little by little, more of our "old self" is rejected and more of our "new self" shines like a beacon to those who are watching.

When the Scriptures were written, there were no chapter divisions and numbered verses. They were more like letters we send to family and friends. When we read the Bible today, we often stop at the end of a chapter. In this case, we need to keep going. After Paul describes the details of our choices to honor God, he gives a beautiful summary that captures our identity and our motivation: "Follow God's example, therefore, as dearly loved children and walk in the way of love, just as Christ loved us and gave himself up for us as a fragrant offering and sacrifice to God" (Eph. 5:1-2). The more the Spirit reveals Christ to our hearts, the more we'll fall in love with Him and follow His example—not out of a teeth-clenching, legalistic determination, but out of delight in His love for us and a sincere desire to please Him. There's a difference . . . a big difference. Even our discipline will be inspired by love.

SENSITIVE HEARTS

As pastors and church leaders, we have the privilege of teaching people about the doors God has opened to the palace. They need to understand how to enjoy all the rooms. If we jump too quickly to the expressions of the spiritual gifts, they may see the Holy Spirit as some kind of electrical current they can plug into. He's not; He's a person, a person who loves, groans, grieves, and delights in those who trust in Christ. As we draw closer to God, we sense more of the emotions of the Spirit living in us. When we sin and grieve Him, we feel His grief. When we repent, we sense His celebration. When we feel hurt or are confused, we know that He groans with deep, loving compassion in us, over us, and through us.

Too many believers and too many church leaders repent out of fear instead of a response to the love of God calling them back to holiness. The Puritan pastor Stephen Charnock describes the stark difference:

> A legalistic conviction of sin arises from a consideration of God's justice chiefly, but an evangelical [gospel-centered] conviction from a sense of God's goodness. A legally convinced person cries out, "I have exasperated a power that is as the roaring of a lion. . . . I have provoked one that is the sovereign Lord of heaven and earth, whose word can tear up the foundation of the world. . . ." But [a person who believes in the kindness and mercy of God] cries, "I have incensed a goodness that is like the dropping of the dew; I have offended a God that had the deportment of a friend."[19]

When the Lord whispers to us in the middle of a conversation or as we're making a decision to avoid gossip and sin, we haven't grieved Him—not yet at least. He's like a loving parent or a faithful friend who is giving us good advice to make a wise choice at that moment. Even when we've made the wrong choices and grieved Him, He doesn't scowl and turn His back on us. He keeps whispering and nudging and reminding us to come back, to be cleansed, healed, and redirected. We don't have to wait until after the conversation or decision to repent. We can stop and do it at any point. For instance, when we're saying things that don't build people up, we can stop and say, "I need to pause right here. Please, forgive me for saying those things. The Spirit just whispered to me that it's wrong for me to talk like that. Let's find a different path for our discussion." When we become sensitive to the Spirit, we welcome His correction at any point.

Have you ever been encouraging a despairing person and felt the Holy Spirit smile within you? That's His joy that we're partnering with Him to care for the young or old, the misfits and outcasts, and the hurting people around us. Have you been in the middle of a conversation when it turned to gossip, and you had a sick feeling in your stomach because you know the loving, tender Spirit of God would never slam anyone like that? That's His gracious conviction and His invitation to repent.

Confidence in the Spirit's kindness and strength opens many doors in the palace. When people are uninformed or afraid, they hide in the foyer, but as they walk into each room and experience more of God, they also see more of their sins. Instead of shame, they learn to become "good repenters," the kind of people who are grateful to be shown sin so that they can experience God's forgiveness even more.

**God opens doors to people at the pace
they choose . . . the speed of their
obedience.**

God opens doors to people at the pace they choose
. . . the speed of their obedience. Some want it all as soon
as they can get it, but others are more cautious. Jesus was
incredibly patient with the disciples. He's no less patient
with us.

THE OTHER ROOMS

All believers—from every denomination and tradition—have come into God's palace and can enjoy all
the comforts, joys, celebrations, and nourishment we've
already described in this chapter. These rooms are magnificent, but they aren't all that God offers. The baptism
in the Spirit opens doors to the other rooms that can't be
accessed by those who haven't had this experience and
aren't growing in the benefits it offers. The first benefit,
as we've seen, is supernatural communication through
the expression of a prayer language. Every Spirit-baptized
believer receives the ability to connect with God in this
way. The second is prophecy. As we've read, Paul tells the
Corinthians to "earnestly desire spiritual gifts, especially
the gift of prophecy" (1 Cor. 14:1). Many people think of
prophecy as "spooky" and strange, but it is given "for edification and exhortation and comfort" (1 Cor. 14:3, NKJV).
That's not weird; that's wonderful!

All the gifts, including the nine Paul lists in his letter to the Corinthians, are given at the Spirit's discretion: "All these are the work of one and the same Spirit, and he distributes them to each one, just as he determines" (1 Cor. 12:11). We don't own them, but we've received instruction and confirmation that these rooms are open to us. We live in our Father's house, and we live to please Him. He directs us into different rooms at different times to find new treasures for different reasons only He knows. We simply walk through the doors God opens for us. We receive the gifts and become stewards of them "for the common good" (1 Cor. 12:7). We trust the Spirit to be our guide, to give us all He wants to give us, and to use us any way He chooses. That's the challenge and the adventure of taking God's hand and walking with Him in humility and power.

Everyone who is baptized in the Spirit will be given a prayer language and many will prophesy; however, not everyone will have the gift of the public expression of tongues or interpretation, words of knowledge or wisdom, faith, discerning spirits, healing, or miracles. God may want to give us these gifts and lead us into new rooms, but they aren't on the radar in many churches. If the baptism in the Spirit has lost its place on the priority list in many churches, these gifts of the Spirit have often vanished almost entirely from our teaching! To reintroduce them, we need clear teaching, effective training, discernment about how God wants to use these gifts, and opportunities to practice them. The investigation, pursuit, and experience of these gifts stimulate sensitivity to God—both for the one practicing the gifts and for those who benefit from them. They give deeper insights into the heart of

God and His purposes for individuals and churches. Using them under God's divine direction inspires and challenges everyone in the congregation. They are, then, fertilizer of growth for everyone involved.

If people want God more than anything else in their lives, He will open many doors. Quite often, God connects available, eager people with particular gifts for specific times, people, and needs. He doesn't waste anything. He waits for us to say, "Lord, I'm listening. I'm ready for anything You have for me." And then He leads us into another room. The Spirit chooses the gifts He wants to give each of us, and we are thrilled with them. In fact, we're thrilled just to be in the palace!

People can learn a lot about these special rooms in the palace, but it's very helpful for them to have a mentor to show them how to be comfortable and useful in each room. These rooms have treasures beyond our imaginations. If people barge in without proper instruction and a humble heart, they'll almost invariably make a mess of things. However, if they have a skilled and patient mentor, they can learn new lessons and find new ways to serve in each room. Mentors help people understand the limits of what they know about the expression of the gifts, as well as prod them to take steps they've never taken before. As pastors learn and grow in leadership skills, we wisely select and train mentors who can help others.

The pastor's role is to teach clearly about all the rooms in the palace, not just the foyer and the living room, and not just the special rooms … all of them. Teaching is crucial, but it's not enough. We need to provide environments for people to ask questions, uncover spiritual blockage and bondage, bathe in God's cleansing flood, experience the baptism in the Spirit, and then learn to live in all the rooms of the palace.

CANDACE'S STORY

We could tell many stories of men and women who have experienced the baptism in the Spirit. All the testimonies are unique, but they all have similarities. We want to let Candace tell her story in her own words:

> My husband and I came to the church needing to heal a lot of hurts we'd experienced in ministry. When we attended a new members' lunch and read the statement of faith, we saw the teaching about the baptism in the Holy Spirit and the evidence of speaking in tongues. Before that day, we'd heard people speak in tongues in services and others interpreted, but all this was new to us.
>
> I started studying the Bible to see what it said about this experience, but I was sure it wasn't for me. I'd trusted in Christ as my Savior when I was six, but when I was twelve, I had some doubts. At that point, I rededicated my life to the Lord. I told Him, "I don't ever want to be at this place of doubt again. I want to drive a stake here and be sure of my salvation. I'm Yours . . . 100 percent." And that's what happened. I believe God anointed and called me to ministry, and He began to use me. By the time my husband and I got to Pastor Scott's church, I'd been serving the Lord for many years. I

never thought I needed anything more from God than what I'd experienced.

As I studied, I had several conversations with Pastor Scott to ask him all kinds of questions. He was very patient as he answered them. No one excluded us or made us feel inferior because we hadn't experienced the baptism in the Spirit. They gave us plenty of room to learn and explore. When we attended church services, I analyzed every syllable I heard as people spoke in tongues and listened to the interpretation. I was sure I heard some kind of patterns, but it still didn't make sense to me.

On a Wednesday night, I was part of the worship team. Pastor Scott taught about the baptism in the Spirit. It confirmed everything he had said to me over the weeks and everything I'd studied, but I didn't feel any drawing to the experience. During the response time, however, we were singing, "Holy Spirit, You are welcome here. Come flood this place. Fill the atmosphere." As we sang, I stopped and prayed, "Holy Spirit, my heart hasn't been a welcoming place to You. I haven't let You flood my life. I invite You to fill any atmosphere in me that You want to fill."

At that moment, the Spirit convicted me that I'd been stubborn and resistant. I thought I was praying silently, "Lord, I'm open to you. Do whatever You want to do in me," but I opened my eyes and realized I was speaking in tongues! I turned off my microphone and sat down on the steps of the stage.

I felt very awkward. I thought about leaving after the service without telling anyone what had happened, but I felt very strongly that the Lord showed me that I needed to tell someone what He was doing in me. I told two people and asked them to pray for me.

On the way home, I tried to replicate the experience, but I couldn't make it happen. I sensed God say to me, "You can keep trying to make it happen again, but it won't work. What happened in the service tonight was real, but what you're doing now isn't."

When I got home, I almost shouted to my husband, "You'll never guess what happened in church tonight."

He smiled, "You spoke in tongues, didn't you?"

I must have looked stunned because he smiled again, "I knew it was going to happen. I just knew it. Anything you tell God you're never going to do, He makes it happen."

The next morning I opened my Bible to read and pray. I told the Lord, "I'm just going to be open to You and see what You have for me." As I prayed, I began speaking in tongues again. After a while, I got quiet, and I prayed, "Lord, if You'd like to interpret my prayer, I would really appreciate it. I'm kind of freaking out, so I'm asking You to tell me what's going on by interpreting my prayer."

I sensed Him say to me, "Look where you are right now."

I answered, "I'm on my bed."

"Yes," He continued, "on your marriage bed. I'm going to reveal something that happened to you when you were thirteen years old."

The Lord showed me an event when I was abused as a little girl. I had suppressed the memory for years, so it came as a surprise to me. Then He assured me, "I'm going to free you from the pain and the damage that event has caused. I'm going to restore passion in your marriage that's been lacking because of this wound. In fact, I'm going to restore passion in every area of your life."

Gradually, God has worked deeply to heal and restore me. I haven't felt ashamed of being abused, and I haven't thought I needed to work hard to earn God's approval. Instead, I've sensed a new depth of His love and forgiveness, and His love has become the source of renewed joy and passion in every relationship and every endeavor. I've let Him love me, and I've simply listened, loved Him in return, and followed His lead.

My husband and I have made a commitment to pray for Pastor Scott and his family. God has used him so powerfully in our lives, and we're thrilled to lift them up to the throne of grace. God often gives me verses of Scripture and prophetic words to send to them. In addition, we've been asked to lead a group in the church. So now, we're serving in a church again, but instead of the church *causing* some of our wounds, God is using this church to *heal* our wounds and give us a platform to minister out of a new wealth of faith, hope, power, and love. It's glorious!

A NEW DAY FOR ALL OF US

As our hearts are filled with the love and power of God, our purposes will be gradually transformed. Increasingly, we'll celebrate with the angels when people come to Christ, we'll weep over broken hearts, families, and bodies, and we'll have a new generosity to give everything we have to His cause—not because anyone is twisting our arms, but because He means more to us than wealth, pleasure, prestige, or popularity. The outpouring of the Spirit began at Pentecost with evangelism as it reached the full range of people at the temple that day. The outpouring of the Spirit continues today as we care more about the lost and the least than our convenience.

When Luke tells us about Jesus' Great Commission to the disciples, he uses a word for "witness" that means "martyr." When we devote ourselves to God and His cause, we pay a price—probably not with our lives, but certainly in comfort, reputation, and resources. When we become His, we make a covenant with Him. Christ gave Himself entirely to us, and we give ourselves entirely to Him. We get the long end of the stick! He got our sins and paid for them on the cross; we get His love, a new identity, and a role in the family enterprise to redeem a lost world! Jesus lived on the razor's edge in His culture. He was severely criticized for loving prostitutes, tax collectors, half-breeds, and unclean misfits. He touched unclean dead people and sick people, the lepers, and the blind. As our hearts are more in tune with His, we'll live on the razor's edge in our culture. We'll love Democrats and Republicans, foreigners and locals, people who speak our language and those who don't, those who sit on the front row in church and the ones on death row. We'll become a little more like Jesus.

Will God ever ask you to do something
you are not able to do? The answer is
yes—all the time! It must be that way, for
God's glory and kingdom. If we function
according to our ability alone, we get
the glory; if we function according to the
power of the Spirit within us, God gets
the glory. He wants to reveal Himself to a
watching world.

—Henry T. Blackaby

CONSIDER THIS . . .

1. What are some fears and doubts that make people
   who have come into the palace feel uncomfortable?
   What gives people confidence and joy to live there?

2. How are you helping people who are "seeking the gifts"? How can you help them more effectively? What difference will it make?

3. How does the use of the gifts affect relationships in the body of Christ? How do they relate to our motivation to reach our Jerusalem, Judea and Samaria, and the ends of the earth?

8 FAN THE FLAME

My fear is not that our great movement . . . will eventually cease to exist or one day die from the earth. My fear is that our people will become content to live without the fire, the power, the excitement, the supernatural element that makes us great.

—John Wesley

As we've said, the vast majority of pastors we know aren't resistant to the work of the Holy Spirit in their lives, not in the least. They believe the doctrines of the nature and work of the Spirit and the importance of the baptism in the Spirit. They find closeness and power in communicating with God in their prayer language. Every time they look up, however, they realize the culture is changing. Technology, mobility, segmentation, and the speed of life have changed modern society. This is an irrefutable fact. The question, then, is, how does the Spirit of God want to work in love, truth, and power in our ever-shifting culture?

NEW WINESKINS

In the middle of Jesus' ministry, the disciples of John the Baptist were confused. Jesus, the Messiah, came just as He was predicted, but not at all the way people expected.

They thought God's Messiah would be a warrior to kick the Romans out of Israel and return the nation to a sovereign, prosperous kingdom. Jesus had a very different agenda. He would reign on earth, but not by military might. The King and His followers would bring a different agenda of love, kindness, sacrifice, and service. Jesus shattered the old assumptions, He taught an astonishing new message, and He modeled a different ethic. Jesus explained to John's disciples that a new container was necessary: "No one sews a patch of unshrunk cloth on an old garment, for the patch will pull away from the garment, making the tear worse. Neither do people pour new wine into old wineskins. If they do, the skins will burst; the wine will run out and the wineskins will be ruined. No, they pour new wine into new wineskins, and both are preserved" (Matt. 9:16-17). Jesus was in the act of replacing traditional thoughts and practices with something new—not totally unrecognizable, but a new way of spiritual life that's supple, flexible, and able to contain the fresh teaching of Jesus.

The changes in our culture require us to take a good, hard look at the wineskins of our traditional practices to see if they're still appropriate. In our case, we're not questioning the message, just the container for delivering the message.

Throughout church history, thoughtful spiritual leaders have wrestled with the questions of connecting ancient truths with modern culture. Some try to move too fast, and some are too resistant. It takes wisdom, patience, and courage to find the right path.

Consider the change in our music over the last several decades. Many of our churches experience "music wars" between proponents of traditional and contemporary songs. This isn't new. Years ago, the hymns of Charles Wesley, Isaac Watts, and Fanny Crosby were brand new. Undoubtedly, there were people who resisted those songs as "too modern" and "not traditional." Today, though, many people consider their songs to be obscure relics of ancient history, like the dinosaurs and the Franco-Prussian War.

The old traditions of teaching the baptism in the Spirit and having tarrying services may still work in some churches. If the old ways work, use them. Pour the wine out for your people to drink deeply and constantly. However, most of us need new wineskins so more people can drink of the Spirit's refreshing love and power. When the old ways became awkward and inconsistent with the modern culture, some of us stopped pouring the wine, or we relegated the wine of the baptism in the Spirit and expressing the gifts to a very small part of church life.

Finding new wineskins is scary business. We're plowing new ground and charting a new course. Inevitably, a number of people won't like it, but for different reasons. Some will accuse us of abdicating our parents' honored traditions, and others will think we've lost our minds to introduce these things in the modern world.

Each of us needs to think biblically, creatively, and culturally to craft a new wineskin for the ministry of the Spirit in our churches. The rapidly changing culture requires more reflection, godly advice, and prayer—not less—so that we craft a wise and workable strategy. Some churches, like The Oaks, have multiple wineskins for different audiences. The worship service at 8:30 in the morning is traditional, but the other services are contemporary.

All of them, though, pour out the wine of the Spirit in ways that nourish people.

No matter the size of your church, ask yourself (and maybe your leaders) these diagnostic questions:

- How has the culture changed in the world, in our community, and in our church?

- What are specific evidences of these changes? How have they affected the expectations of people in our church and our community?

- How many of our leaders are flowing in the gifts of the Spirit?

- How and when are the expressions of the Spirit manifested in our church?

- When and how can we teach the nature and role of the Holy Spirit and the baptism in the Spirit?

- How are our leaders and church members being mentored in all aspects of spiritual life?

These are difficult questions that require careful thought and serious discussions. Quite often, the answers surface slowly in prayer, in conversations with other leaders in the church, and with friends and mentors who love us enough to engage us at a deep level of insight and honesty.

IT BEGINS WITH YOU

Many pastors have legitimate fears about inaugurating change. They've been blasted when they've tried to make changes before, and they don't want to go through that again! Some changes, though, aren't optional. They're necessary if we're going to accomplish the purposes of God. To face the almost inevitable pushback, we need to ask God to stir up the fire in us. We pray, "O God, inflame the desire in my heart that every person in our community will know You and experience all You have for them. Break my heart over their brokenness, and give me the thrill of seeing lives radically changed. Lord, use me to lead people to the palace. Use me to take people into the family room and the kitchen so they feel safe, secure, loved, and well fed. And Lord, use me to open the doors to Your treasures through the baptism in the Spirit and the experience of tongues and the other gifts." Some of us may need to also pray, "Lord, forgive me for letting my passion fade and for failing to teach the ways of the Spirit with boldness. I'm ready now."

When we pray like this, some of us quickly realize that we've sung lyrics, like "Holy Spirit, You are welcome here," but we haven't opened every door to Him in our own lives. We may need to ask ourselves why we've been complacent about communicating these truths to our people when they were so meaningful to us in the past.

One of the concerns I (Scott) had about creating a new wineskin for our church was that I needed to learn how to teach, train, and lead more effectively in the baptism in the Spirit and in the follow-up with those who received it. When I began changing the culture of our church, I realized that too many people still felt pressured. I hadn't taught them well enough, so they felt manipulated when I invited them to receive the baptism in the Spirit. A major part of my learning curve was the process of analyzing my communication and changing my message so people sensed the warmth of God's inviting hand instead of hearing only a demand. First, I had to look into my own heart and uncover the pressure I felt so I could let God heal me and change me. Then I could relax, teach more clearly, and patiently invite people to respond to God's loving touch.

A major part of my learning curve was the process of analyzing my communication and changing my message so people sensed the warmth of God's inviting hand instead of hearing only a demand.

The first step for pastors is to pray, to trust God to give them more passion and clarity than they've ever had before, and to ask Him for a strategy to create a new wineskin in their churches.

STRATEGIC STEPS WITH LEADERS

The strategy doesn't begin with a huge campaign with posters, grand announcements, a sermon series, and handouts. The next step is to simply tell our leaders about our experience of being baptized in the Spirit and our growing thirst for God. We can then invite them to share their stories and ask questions. These conversations need to take place more than every decade or two! If the work of the Spirit is central to our lives and ministries, we'll stimulate a lot of wonderful discussions on all levels.

Some of your leaders may wonder what took you so long, and some may fear that you're going to wreck the church because you'll be culturally irrelevant. Be patient and persistent. Teach, train, and model the life of the Spirit in your meetings. Begin each board meeting by praying in the Spirit and inviting them to pray in the Spirit at the same time. You'll probably need to explain what's going on and coach them as they begin this practice. It will add richness to your relationships because together, you're connecting with the heart of God.

Communicating with God doesn't happen *before* your agenda; it *is* your agenda. You'll still talk about finances, building, groups, children's ministry, youth group, and everything else, but you and the board can pray in the Spirit about all these things. At every point, ask God what He wants to do in those areas of ministry and in particular people's lives. Teach and model what it means to "pray in the Spirit at all times" (Eph. 6:18).

Your leaders will soon realize your goal isn't just to get people to speak in tongues. Instead, they'll understand that the new wineskin is about experiencing the life of the Spirit in every way by everyone at all times. The palace is huge and beautiful. Every room is full of God's love and strength, the fellowship of other believers, and all the resources we could ever need.

INTRODUCING THE NEW WINESKIN

When your leaders experience the fullness of the Spirit and realize the presence of God in fresh and real ways, they'll long for every person in the church to have the same experience. They'll help craft the strategy for the new wineskin, and they'll support it every step of the way. There are, of course, many questions:

- Where, when, and how will you teach people about the person and work of the Holy Spirit?

- When is the best time to invite people to be baptized in the Spirit?

- What kind of follow-up will help them grow and learn to use their prayer language and the other gifts?

- Who will shepherd them?

- What are the venues where the gifts can be expressed?

- How will you introduce the expression of the gifts in these services?

- How will you assure your leaders and the people that everything will be done decently and in order?

- How will you discern the Enemy's schemes to knock you off balance and off message?

- What do you need to do to stay fresh and strong during the change in culture?

Many pastors could benefit from a tested curriculum that can be taught in groups, classes, and even services. Look for a body of teaching that fits the needs of your new wineskin, and make any adjustments that may be necessary for it to be most effective.

Leadership is both art and science. We need wisdom to craft a good strategy, but we also need relational skills to inform, motivate, and shepherd people to drink from the new wineskins.

Leadership is both art and science. We need wisdom to craft a good strategy, but we also need relational skills to inform, motivate, and shepherd people to drink from the new wineskins. Welcome questions, even the ones you've answered a dozen times before. You'll need to make plenty of adjustments along the way to fine-tune the new strategy so that it works well and to respond to the continuing changes in the culture. Through it all, you're never alone. The Spirit of God delights that you want to lead people into every room in the palace. He's your Advocate, Comforter, and Helper.

YOU'RE READY

Pastors, you have the fire of God in you. Feed it until it consumes you and until countless others are ignited by your flame. In Paul's last letter before he was executed, he knew his protégé was struggling, so he gave Timothy strong encouragement:

> For this reason I remind you to fan into flame the gift of God, which is in you through the laying on of my hands. For the Spirit God gave us does not make us timid, but gives us power, love and self-discipline. So do not be ashamed of the testimony about our Lord or of me his prisoner. Rather, join with me in suffering for the gospel, by the power of God. (2 Tim. 1:6-8)

Paul was telling Timothy, "You've got the fire in you, but it's smoldering. Stir it up! Fan it into a raging fire again! Don't doubt, and don't be shy. The Spirit gives us everything we need to represent God, in good times and in hard times. Even when we suffer—*especially* when we suffer—we depend on the power of God to work in us and through us to accomplish His kingdom-building, kingdom-expanding purposes."

At times, all of us are like Timothy. Discouragement, heartache, exhaustion, criticism, and a dozen other factors can cause our flame to flicker. We need someone like Paul to put a hand on our shoulders and say, "Hey, God has your back. You can trust Him. In fact, He has more for you than you can imagine. Trust Him. More than ever, trust Him."

At times, we need this encouragement, and at times, the people around us need it. We're all thoroughly human. We waver, we balk, and we stumble, and the fire grows dim for a while. Don't let it stay dim. Find a friend to be like

Paul for you—and be like Paul to those around you. Live in freedom and boldness in the palace, show your people how to live in all the rooms, and invite people from all over your community and the world to join you there.

You said yes to God's Spirit long ago, and hopefully, the message of this book has confirmed all He has been doing in your life and ministry. However, if you're like many of us, you sense the tug of the Spirit to fan the flame again. You realize there's more. He's waiting for you, and He's smiling. Jesus promised, "Signs will accompany those who believe": divine power, communication, protection, and healing (Mark 16:15-18). If we proclaim the gospel of grace and truth, He promises to work in us, with us, and through us and to confirm His Word with these signs. Jesus ascended to heaven, but He sent His Spirit to do even more because the laborers were multiplied. Mark tells us, "Then the disciples went out and preached everywhere, and the Lord worked with them and confirmed his word by the signs that accompanied it" (Mark 16:20).

The Lord is still making this offer to us today. Imagine the excitement the disciples experienced when they saw God's promises come true! Imagine the "crowd of witnesses" described in Hebrews 12 as they watch us and cheer us on as we believe the promises and step out in faith!

This is our prayer for you:

God, we pray over those who have just read this book. Give them a sense of expectancy that You will do great things in and through them. We ask You to do fresh things among them. May Your

Spirit guide and empower them. Make the truth of Your Word come alive as they read it, study it, and teach it. O Lord, break any spirit of fear and doubt. Give them fresh faith and a rekindled fire. We pray their leaders will embrace You and all You want to do in their churches. We look to You. We depend on You. We love you. We give You all honor and thanks in Jesus' name. Amen.

Take care of giving up your first zeal; beware of cooling in the least degree. You were hot and earnest once; be hot and earnest still, and let the fire which once burned within you still animate you. Be still men of might and vigor, men who serve their God with diligence and zeal.

—Charles Spurgeon

CONSIDER THIS . . .

1. How does the concept of "new wineskins" apply to crafting our communication to the modern culture?

2. What are the benefits of starting the strategy by teaching and modeling for church leaders before any church-wide communication?

3. When does a pastor or church leader need to "fan into
    flame the gift of God"? What are some ways that can
    happen?

ENDNOTES

1. Cited in a resolution by the South Texas AG District Council, "Reaffirmation of the Pentecostal Distinctive: The Initial Physical Evidence of the Holy Spirit Baptism."

2. "Holding Their Tongues: The Assemblies of God asks whether its distinctive teaching is being lost in outreach efforts," Cary McMullen, *Christianity Today*, September 21, 2009.

3. "Fire," *Baker's Evangelical Dictionary of Biblical Theology* (Grand Rapids: Baker Books, 1966), www.biblestudytools.com/dictionaries/bakers-evangelical-dictionary/fire.html

4. "Why Do These Pentecostals Keep Growing?" Ed Stetzer, *Christianity Today*, November 11, 2014, www.christianitytoday.com/edstetzer/2014/november/why-are-pentecostals-growing.html

5. Vinson Synan, *The Century of the Holy Spirit: 100 years of Pentecostal and Charismatic Renewal, 1901–2001* (Nashville: Thomas Nelson Publishers, 2001), 42–45.

6. 2013 ACMR Report, http://ag.org/top/About/statistics/index.cfm

7. Dick Brogden, AG Centennial Celebration, posted August 12, 2014, 100.ag.org/video/dick-brogden-ag-celebration/

8. Cited in "The Six People Americans Now Trust More than Their Pastor," Kate Tracy, *Christianity Today*, December 16, 2013.

9. Roger Stronstad, *The Charismatic Theology of St. Luke* (Ada, Michigan: Baker Academic Books, 2012), 81.

10. Though the verses at the end of Mark are missing from some early manuscripts, they are found in others, including those known as A, C, and D. There was evidently a copyist's error in the first or second century. However, church fathers, such as Irenaeus, were familiar with this ending of Mark. The passage is consistent with the endings of the other gospels and found in important manuscripts, so we can be confident in its authenticity.

11. "Have We Forgotten the Power of Touch?" Nicole Watt, *Christianity Today*, June 2014.

12. Jim Cymbala, *Fresh Wind, Fresh Fire* (Grand Rapids: Zondervan, 1997), 147.

13. Donald Gee, *Toward Pentecostal Unity* (Springfield: Gospel Publishing House, 1961), 18.

14. For more on how to train leaders and church members in using the gifts, read *Clear the Stage* by Scott Wilson and John Bates.

15. R. A. Torrey, *How To Pray* (London: Oliphants, 1955), 40.

16. William Booth, *Salvation Soldiery: A Series of Addresses on the Requirements of Jesus Christ's Service* (Charleston, SC: Nabu Press, 2014), 141.

17. For the "Rules of Engagement," see *Clear the Stage* by Scott Wilson and John Bates, or download this document by going to core.theoaksonline.org

18. For more on the Core and the Freedom Quest, see *Clear the Stage* by Scott Wilson and John Bates.

19. Stephen Charnock, *The Complete Works of Stephen Charnock, Vol. 4* (Amazon Digital Services, Inc., 2010), 199.

ACKNOWLEDGEMENTS

We are so grateful for the encouragement, insights, and feedback from many people.

Thank you, Dr. George Wood and Dr. Jim Bradford, for your input and encouragement on this project. We love and respect you so much.

Thank you, Sol and Wini Arledge and Steve and Susan Blount, for asking us to write the book and guiding us every step of the way.

Thank you, Chris Railey, Heath Adamson, and Justin Lathrop, for being our sounding boards and wise advisors.

Thank you, Dr. Paul Brooks, for the hours you put into this book. We deeply appreciate your expertise and wisdom. We are also grateful for the hours of prayers and support you've shown us as we've lived out of this book in real time. You are an inspiration.

Thank you, Pat Springle, for working with us to craft this book. You are such a phenomenal gift to the church and to both of us. We love and appreciate the synergy that occurred the moment you walked into the room with us. We are forever grateful.

Thank you to the faithful staff members and elders of The Oaks Fellowship and Freedom Fellowship International for your love, prayers, and support.

Thank you, God, for friendships that makes us sharper and for never giving up on us.

ABOUT THE AUTHORS

SCOTT WILSON

Scott Wilson has been in fulltime pastoral ministry for more than twenty-five years. He is the senior pastor of The Oaks Fellowship, located in Dallas, Texas—now ministering to 3,000 people each week.

Scott is the author of several books, including *Ready, Set, Grow*; *Act Normal*; *The Next Level*; and *Steering Through Chaos*. He and John are co-authors of *Clear the Stage*.

Scott and his wife, Jenni, have three boys: Dillon, Hunter, and Dakota. The Wilsons live in the Dallas area.

JOHN BATES

John Bates has been in full-time ministry since 1986. He accepted his second lead pastor position in 2003 at Freedom Fellowship International in Waxahachie, Texas. The church is prophetic in nature, abundant in resources, free in worship, and large in purpose, and submitted to the leadership of the Holy Spirit.

There is a deep love for taking the truth to the nations at FFI. As a result, John has ministered through crusades and pastoral leadership seminars in Central and Latin America, the Caribbean, Africa, and Asia, as well as extensively throughout Europe.

Due to his focus on discipleship, John has created Freedom Quest, consisting of a two-day Carpe Diem (seize the day) encounter with God. This event is followed by an intensive twelve-week mentorship. The results are men and women learning to experience freedom in Christ and learning how to walk said freedom out successfully.

Under John's leadership, FFI is now known as a praying church and sends teams throughout the world to conduct and lead prophetic prayer events. Prayer is the directing factor in John's life and ministry. John is co-author with Scott Wilson of *Clear the Stage*.

John and his wife, Shelli, live in the Dallas area where they parent Nehemiah, Eden, and their dog Cookie.

FOR MORE INFORMATION

For more information about these and other helpful resources, visit www.myhealthychurch.com

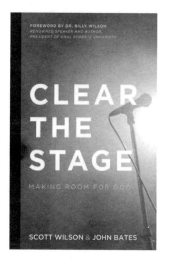

Clear the Stage: Can your church be both seeker-friendly and spirit-filled? In *Clear the Stage*, Scott Wilson and John Bates share how God gave them a vision to marry these two divergent streams of church practice. You don't have to choose between the old revivalist mentality and the more recent seeker-friendly plan. Instead, the authors present a whole new way of doing church that clears the stage so the Spirit of God can do what only He can.

Ready, Set, Grow: Over a three-year-period, Wilson walked with his staff through a three-stage development process: modeling (year 1), mentoring (year 2), and multiplying (year 3). First, he writes, leaders must develop their own leadership capacities and become someone worth following. Then, they must lead their direct reports (whether staff or volunteer) through a similar developmental process. Finally, they need to create an environment where their direct reports are developing the people in their domain of ministry. A healthy church doesn't have to be a huge church, but it does need to be a growing church. *Ready, Set, Grow* will help you understand how to lead your church/ministry through a process of personal and organizational growth.

Act Normal: A thirty-one-day journey through the book of Acts, each day's reading discusses what it means to live for God and be empowered by the Holy Spirit. By expressing complex concepts in everyday language and using real-life examples, Scott Wilson helps you grasp the story that runs through Acts and teaches you how to live in a way that honors God.

The Next Level: Learn to see the tests of life from God's perspective. Your times of pain and confusion aren't meant to be prisons that keep you from enjoying life. Instead, God wants to use them as classrooms to teach you the most valuable lessons you can ever learn.

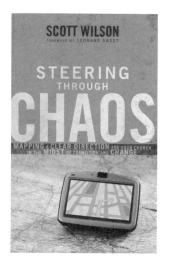

Steering Through Chaos: The challenges of leadership often multiply during times of transition. *Steering through Chaos* helps church leaders plan for change by developing a communication strategy, enlisting support, and building momentum to lead their staffs and congregations through transition. This book provides the insight, inspiration, and courage you need to make the difficult choices that will keep your church moving forward.